PENGUIN BOOKS

Funny Girls

Diane Atkinson curated the *Fawcett's Funny Girls – Cartooning for Equality* exhibition. She was also responsible for the revisionist exhibition about the Suffragettes, *The Purple, White and Green: Suffragettes in London 1906–14*, held at the Museum of London in 1992, which travelled to New Zealand in 1993 and Australia in 1994 to celebrate their respective centenaries of women's suffrage. Her Ph.D. was on the politics of women's sweated labour. She has published *The Suffragettes in Pictures* (1996), a book of around two hundred suffragette photographs, and her book on Kitty Marion, the actor, suffragette and birth control campaigner, is forthcoming.

Funny Girls

Cartooning for Equality

Diane Atkinson

This book is to be returned on or before the last date stamped below or you will be charged a fine

PENGUIN BOOKS

Published by the Penguin Group
Penguin Books Ltd, 27 Wrights Lane, London W8 5TZ, England
Penguin Books USA Inc., 375 Hudson Street, New York, New York 10014, USA
Penguin Books Australia Ltd, Ringwood, Victoria, Australia
Penguin Books Canada Ltd, 10 Alcorn Avenue, Toronto, Ontario, Canada M4V 3B2
Penguin Books (NZ) Ltd, 182–190 Wairau Road, Auckland 10, New Zealand

Penguin Books Ltd, Registered Offices: Harmondsworth, Middlesex, England

Published in 1997
10 9 8 7 6 5 4 3 2 1

Set in 11/13.5pt Monotype Bembo
Designed in QuarkXpress on an Apple Macintosh
Printed in England by Clays Ltd, St Ives plc

For Patrick Hughes.

Contents

Illustrations

Acknowledgements

The author would like to thank: James Cupper, David Doughan, Catherine Penn and Veronica Perkins at the Fawcett Library, London Guildhall University; Miranda Taylor at the Punch Library; Rob Edwards and Jane Newton at the Centre for the Study of Cartoons and Caricature, University of Kent; the Cartoon Art Trust; Cath Tate of Cath Tate Cards; Carol Bennet of FANNY; Les Coleman; Thomas Kibling; Dr Anne Summers; and the Carl Ronald Giles Trust. Special thanks to Mark Bryant and Simon Heneage for their invaluable *Dictionary of British Cartoonists and Caricaturists, 1730–1980* (Scolar Press, 1994).

Thank you also to: the *Daily Mail* for permission to quote an extract from the Peter Lewis article on pp. 28–9 and from the 'Fighting Mad: The Ford's Wives' article on p. 82; the *Evening Standard* for permission to quote an extract of the 'Corrisande' article on pp. 20–21 and the 'Fair Play for Husbands' article on pp. 76–7; and Faber and Faber Ltd for permission to quote from Philip Larkin's poem 'This Be The Verse', from *High Windows*, on p. 99, copyright © the Estate of Philip Larkin, 1974.

Fawcett would also like to thank the following for permission to use the cartoons and illustrations listed below: the Mary Evans Picture Library for 2; the Fawcett Library/London Guildhall University for 10, 12, 13, 29 and 55; Punch Limited for 3, 8, 14, 18, 24, 30, 31, 33, 38, 43, 47, 54, 62, 67, 68 and 69; Diane Atkinson for 5; the Museum of London for 6; Mirror Group Newspapers for 7, 19, 59 and 60; Irene Cockcroft for 9; the Speaker's Office for 11; Solo/*Evening Standard* for 15, 16, 36 and 57; the Labour Party Archive for 17; Ronald Searle for 20; *Daily Mail* for 21 and 35, Telegraph Group Limited for 22 and 51; Viv Quillin for 23, 41 and 72; Posy Simmonds for 25, 44, 64 and 75; Ros Asquith for 26 and 50; Cath Tate Cards for 27 and 42; Solo for 37; Liberty for 39; Jo Harvatt for 40; Kate Charlesworth for 28, 48 and 52; Günter Böhmer Collection for 45 and 46; Jacky Fleming for 49, 53, 77, 79 and 80; Bernard Crossley for 56; Solo/*Daily Mail* for 61; MoD Army (Recruiting) for 63; Claire Calman for 65 and 66; Musée du Louvre (Photo AKG2/MI20/VI/10/6) for 70; Paula

Youens for 71; Christine Roche for 73; Caroline Firenza for 74; and Rona Chadwick for 78.

All reasonable inquiries have been made to ascertain the identity and whereabouts of all persons authorized to permit the reproduction of the cartoons, illustrations and text extracts included. In the few cases where we have not been successful, should the identity of such persons come to light after publication of this book, we will take all reasonable steps to make appropriate acknowledgements and to negotiate permission.

The views expressed in this book do not necessarily represent the policy of Fawcett.

Foreword

by Betty Boothroyd, MP, Speaker of the House of Commons

Cartoons seem a silly subject for a serious person like me, a Member of Parliament, indeed the Speaker of the House of Commons, its referee and representative. They are the light bits marooned in the facts and reports and opinions of the newspapers, just glanced at, then we pass on to the serious stuff. But through pictures we can understand change in another way. We have all seen those photographs of our grandparents and our parents, and what a different time that seems. When I look back at those photographs of me electioneering in the Fifties and Sixties, it seems an age ago. Pictures illustrate a story so much more fully than mere words. And the pictures in this book are more than photographs, they are images selected by the artists, drawn and re-drawn, to make a strong point through humour.

I was drawn to the rich subject of humour and politics, oddly enough, by the suffragettes, those fierce and, one might suppose, not funny feminists. I went to see *The Purple, White and Green: Suffragettes in London 1906–1914* at the Museum of London in 1992 and I was humbled to be in the presence of those brave women who went to prison for the vote. Many of them went on hunger-strike and endured force-feeding so that women could be part of the political process. One of the things that I learnt, or re-learnt, was that the suffragettes used humour and drawings a lot to try and change attitudes.

A cartoon can encapsulate ideas: I have been cartooned myself, and sometimes I can even recognize Betty Boothroyd! The cartoons in this book, divided as they are into three themes: 'Politics and Power', 'Work', and 'Sharing the Caring', are arranged historically. They give an idea of how society has changed, is changing, and should be changed. Laugh, smile, wryly grin, but remember our first step is to understand society; the second step is to change it.

My own experience resonates particularly with the first section of the book. The cartoon on this page suggests the Edwardians' idea of hell: Mrs Speaker. I am that vision come true. The culture and hours of Westminster make it a challenge to be a woman Member of Parliament, and an even greater challenge if you have children. Sadly, sometimes voters mistrust a woman who takes up a career in politics, and

1. Detail of 'The Suffragette's Vision: Mrs Speaker', Anon., Raphael Tuck and Sons, 1912.

who has a family, and judge her harshly. I certainly believe that if I had been married and had a family I would never have made this cartoon become a reality. I hope the strong messages which have been drawn in this book encourage women to realize their own dreams, and inspire the futures of others.

Preface

by Shelagh Diplock, Director of the Fawcett Society

Millicent Garrett Fawcett at the age of twenty-two set out on the first speaking tour of her sixty-year-long campaign for women's suffrage. She would list the many reasons given as to why women could not be given the vote. It was said that women were intellectually inferior. They were physically inferior. They were too pure to be involved in politics. If given the vote, they would neglect their families and homes. Men would no longer open doors for them. Women did not really want the vote, and so on.

Then, one by one, she would demolish these points, using her sharp logical mind and quick wit. This powerful mix of reasoned arguments to promote a cause, combined with humour to keep the audience listening, remains a most effective strategy to this day.

The newspaper cartoon encapsulates this process. A cartoon can get a message across, sometimes a very complex, subtle or uncomfortable message, by breaking down defensiveness and making the reader laugh.

2. Millicent Garrett Fawcett, leader of the National Union of Women's Suffrage Societies, c. 1892.

It is therefore very appropriate that the modern Fawcett Society, one hundred and thirty years later, should choose an exhibition of cartoons about women to illustrate the history of their long march towards equality.

Many of the arguments used to deny women the vote came up again and again every time women pushed forward for new rights or opportunities. The right to own or earn for themselves, to be educated and to hold power in their own right. It is a mark of the progress women have made that at the end of the twentieth century these earlier arguments have at last been consigned to the extremist fringes of the debate and are no longer taken seriously.

Although the principle of equality between women and men has largely been won, the reality of many women's lives illustrates that in practical terms women still remain one or more steps behind men in many ways. For instance, in the home: attitude surveys show that a large majority of women and men agree that domestic and caring responsibilities should be shared. However, these same surveys reveal that only two out of ten men take a real share of the work in the home. Women are in the workplace in increasing numbers. However, most women still work in undervalued, low-paid or low-status part-time jobs. Even women at the top of their professions tend to be paid less than men. And, of course, a woman gaining a top post in public or business life is still treated as headline news and a male-dominated Parliament has more men named John than it has women MPs.

The suffrage movement blazed the trail for modern campaigners to follow. The Fawcett Society, which had turned to campaigning for equality in employment after the vote was won, played an active part in the post-war feminist campaigns, for equal rights and pay, and sex equality laws, which flourished in the Sixties and Seventies. However, Fawcett's future as a campaign organization came under pressure from the very changes in women's lives that it had helped to bring about.

Women took advantage of new work and life opportunities and found themselves in the era of 'superwoman'. The pressure on middle-class women to succeed at work and also be a perfect homemaker, wife and mother took its toll. It began to seem that women had merely won the right to be exhausted. Working-class women continued to have to struggle just to make ends meet. Juggling work and home certainly left little time and energy for campaigning.

Many young women, having grown up in a new atmosphere of equal rights, are wondering what all the fuss was about. They take for granted that they have the same capabilities and opportunities as men. They are not willing to accept unfair treatment or harassment at work, and when they become mothers, they are looking for practical support to balance work and home. They do not want to be made to feel guilty whatever they choose to do, paid work or full-time motherhood. They want to be valued as women, as mothers, as individuals.

To meet the new challenges, Fawcett has been reorganized and transformed into a modern pressure group. With a growing membership and a new groups network backed up by a talented team producing lively and effective campaigns, we are successfully getting women's priorities on to the agenda of politicians and decision-makers.

This book and the exhibition from which it is derived will bring the messages to the attention of a new generation of supporters, young and old. We celebrate the achievements of the past, remind ourselves of the barriers which remain, and look forward to creating a changed world in which both men and women are able to balance their work and home lives and support each other in equal partnership.

Introduction

Fawcett's Funny Girls – Cartooning for Equality has been a delightful exhibition to work on, and I have particularly enjoyed choosing the images and researching the artists and their times. But this book, which includes a selection of the best cartoons, has been more difficult to write because ephemeral jokes can easily be killed by the kindness of attending to them for more than a moment. They can be disinterred, but still not brought back to life. Dissection happens after death, to find out how things work: so I apologize in advance if some of these jokes die on the page. I have tried not to be solemn, I have tried not to be a pedantic old bat. What I want to do is to point out the relevance of these pictures; and to bring them back to life by shining the light of their times on them, and projecting the jokes into our own time.

Fawcett's Funny Girls has also been a tricky exhibition to work on. I have waded through a hundred and thirty years of dusty newspapers, looking at badly drawn cartoons with badly written captions about the incomprehensible 'ishoos' of their times. I have been the victim of more unfunny jokes than the chairman of a working men's club. There is nothing so old as yesterday's newspaper. I decided to tell the story of the way attitudes have changed over the last hundred and thirty years – or not – and how the jokes have rebounded on the comedians.

Shelagh Diplock, Director of the Fawcett Society, thought it would be useful to examine the cartoons under three headings: 'Politics and Power', 'Work' and 'Sharing the Caring': and this has proved to be a most interesting way into the two very disparate worlds of feminism and cartoons. Nowadays feminist cartooning is an honourable occupation with a history and a rationale, stars and foot-soldiers. However, although there are as many men as women cartoonists included in this book, over the period we are looking at the great majority of cartoonists have been men. And this is still true of cartoonists today.

I have squeezed a John Leech cartoon from *Punch* of 1853 into the section 'Politics and Power', because it features a woman MP, a bizarre, almost surrealistic image to the mid-Victorians; but she is working behind piles of documents at her desk so it could have been considered under the rubric of 'Work'; and, since she has a family of eight children

I

and a bewhiskered husband, the cartoonist could also have been addressing the subject of 'Sharing the Caring'. What I hope you will do as a reader is think about these cartoons in the bit of light I can throw on them, but also in the light of your own experience and interests. I cannot, and would not want to, read these cartoons for you: I have tried to help by suggesting some of the meanings I can tease out of them. My readings are meant as pointers on your own journey. The three categories cover major themes in women's thinking and agitation this century, and they remain as important and critical for women today and tomorrow.

My selection of cartoons is just the tip of a mountain of drawings. With an average of ten daily papers coming out every year, each featuring sometimes as many as five cartoons, and countless weeklies, monthlies and other periodicals being published, there must have been very roughly half a million cartoons produced during this time, and I sometimes feel as if I have looked at all of them. Mine is a tiny sample of this discourse. There is a lot of journeyman work here: material included largely because it illustrates the topic; or because it is particularly bad or silly. There are no works of genius: nothing by Saul Steinberg or Charles Addams or 'Anton', that brilliant sister and brother team. But there are works of huge talent by Posy Simmonds, and Giles, and Osbert Lancaster, and Kate Charlesworth, alongside cartoons which have a myriad other virtues.

Jokes do not lie on the page, though they can die on the page. The joke first explodes in the cartoonist's head, and then she flings it on to the paper, hoping it will bounce from there into your head. But sometimes the jokes die, and my remarks bury them. The cartoonist may have been a funny old chap in Edwardian England – how can his idea live on in your mind for a moment? He craves your indulgence. I ask you to look as a critic and feel as a woman, and smile when you can.

Cartoonists are artists working alone, trying to illustrate issues by metaphoric, symbolic and other story-telling means. They do not always have a point of view of their own, sometimes the drawing is simply an illustration of the opposing views of the day, and the reader is presumed to know what is the right thinking on that particular issue. Which may be the opposite of how we right-thinking people think now.

This book only includes cartoons which have been published.

2

Consider for a moment those poor little cartoons that saw the light of day for about a week or two – enough time to get to the Editor's desk and then to be rejected, chucked in the waste-paper basket. What a book that would be! We can imagine a perfect book of dazzling insights, brilliant drawings, very, very funny. But that book can only exist in our imagination. I was dealing with the real world when I made this selection. This is why it is social history and not art history. This selection is of work that artists and editors agreed was part of the debate.

Funny Girls can be read four ways: as pictures; for their captions; for my prose accompaniment; and under the overall headlines. Whichever way you read it, the story is the story of women and their progress through this century.

A poignant source of comedy has always been, since the Greeks, and notably in the Renaissance, 'the world turned upside-down'. The catalogue of the exhibition *The Topsy-Turvy World* (first seen at the Goethe Institute, Amsterdam, in 1984) has helped me get a handle on one of the main mechanisms of the 'joke-work', as Freud called it. In the world turned upside-down you can reverse cause and effect, human and animal, male and female. The crossing of boundaries which takes place during the festival of Saturn, and on All Fools' Day, when animals are brought into the church, and masters wait on their servants, is a licence to show the workings of social order. A great theme in the cartoons included in this selection is the reversal of roles. It is often accepted that the male and the female roles are both given, and that men naturally behave like men, and women like women. But the reversal of roles is in the end an irrelevance: women do not want to be men, they want to be women with power.

1 | Politics and Power

Mary Wollstonecraft and Millicent Garrett Fawcett knew that the route to power was through politics. Demonstrations, journalism and the ballot box have won a great victory for women in the last hundred and thirty years. At least as much again remains to be done: but education for all, universal suffrage and equal pay are milestones in women's liberation. There remains the massive personal, psychological and biological issue of children, which women are uniquely structured to bear, and for whom they have been historically condemned to care. Considered in the context of the lives of billions of women, past and present, these few scratchy little drawings seem a feeble signal. But in the light of our endeavours and ambitions they help us to understand how we got where we are, and why we have not got any further yet, and how we might yet get our fair share.

Cartoonists deal in stereotypes: fine artists deal in reality and imagination, but journalism demands headlines, short-cuts and slogans. Psychologically people deal in stereotypes too. Men judge women by their mother, the Queen, pornography, or Hollywood and other superficialities. What the cartoonist does at her best is to take some fool's stereotype and show it for what it is: a shallow simplification, a colossal misunderstanding, a malign vision which ignores real people in favour of prejudices. Over the period covered by the exhibition the drawings change in style, a shorthand develops in the modern manner, but the enemies are still the same: myopic thinking and reactionary attitudes. When the cartoonist sits down to draw, she wants to change something. The drawing on the page is merely the wall of the squash court: the players – the cartoonist and her reader – are hitting the ball of thought back and forth between each other. The cartoon is the mirror that reflects to the reader what its author is saying. It might be difficult for us to project ourselves back to seemingly distant times like the beginning of the century, for instance, but if the idea is strong enough it will still bounce off a soft wall or shine through a faded mirror, and it will invade our consciousness for a moment.

The suffragettes and the suffragists (often the same people) fought for the vote and gained universal suffrage. Their tremendous visual and verbal campaign won the battle. The hateful First World War is a red herring in the story of women's political development. Women did not get the vote because they filled artillery shells, they got the vote because right was on their side. The feeble politicians of the day kept putting up a straight bat but they were on a sticky wicket and they were bound to get bowled out sooner rather than later. It has been an enormous disappointment to idealists that the vote for women has not made a big difference. However, realists will realize that the vote was first of all a symbolic victory: now women have to use their power.

THE PARLIAMENTARY FEMALE.

Father of the Family. "COME. DEAR; WE SO SELDOM GO OUT TOGETHER NOW—CAN'T YOU TAKE US ALL TO THE PLAY TO-NIGHT!"

Mistress of the House, and M.P. "HOW YOU TALK, CHARLES! DON'T YOU SEE THAT I AM TOO BUSY. I HAVE A COMMITTEE TO-MORROW MORNING, AND I HAVE MY SPEECH ON THE GREAT CROCHET QUESTION TO PREPARE FOR THE EVENING."

By trying to imagine a female Member of Parliament, John Leech is opening the debate sixty-six years before the fact. Aware of the brewing feminist and suffragist ferment, *Punch* devoted its 1853 Almanack to 'The Ladies of Creation', who seemed intent on the most disturbing reversal of roles. The debate about the vote was actually about the gender of the voters and not the sex of the Member of Parliament. The cartoon is a parody of another scene: when we transpose the heads of the Mistress of the House and the Father of the Family, the subject is trivial. The problem with which she is struggling, 'The Great Crotchet Question', underlines the ludicrousness of the idea of a woman Member of Parliament.

In 1851 Harriet Taylor (1807–58), the wife of John Stuart Mill, described in the *Westminster Review* the agitation for the vote by her American 'sisters'. Their first public meeting was in Ohio in 1850, followed soon after by a 'Women's Rights Convention' in Massachusetts, a movement she said was 'not merely *for* women but *by* them'. Two key resolutions passed at the Convention were: 'That women are entitled to the rights of suffrage, and to be considered eligible to office' and 'That civil and political rights acknowledge no sex, and therefore the word "male" should be struck from every State Constitution'. Despite the urgings of Harriet Taylor, the British women's suffrage movement did not start to organize until the 1860s. Its approach would be constitutional: collecting petitions demanding the vote, lobbying for support from local Members of Parliament, and holding garden parties and drawing-room meetings. In 1897 the National Union of Women's Suffrage Societies (NUWSS) was formed, and Millicent Garrett Fawcett was its President.

John Leech (1817–64) cartooned for *Punch* almost from its first issue in 1841. He started to train as a doctor but had to give up his studies when his father went bankrupt. He was influenced by Honoré Daumier, had no formal art training, but was taught to etch by George Cruikshank, another caricaturist.

3. (Left) John Leech, *Punch*, 1853.

4. The head of the long-suffering husband transposed on to the shoulders of his politician wife: husband and wife restored to their 'true' roles.

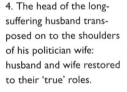

Five scrawny, ill-tempered and over-dressed shrews are the stereotypical image of the suffragettes who fought the militant campaign for the vote. They are old maids, past the flush of youth, three are boss-eyed and aggressive, with umbrella and handbag as weapons. They are bitter and twisted.

John Hassall's postcard illustrates a poem originally published in *Punch* in 1870:

> The rights of Women who demand,
> Those women are but few:
> The greater part had rather stand
> Exactly as they do.
>
> Beauty has claims, for which she fights
> At ease, with winning arms;
> The women who want women's rights
> Want, mostly, Woman's charms.

Hassall's vision of suffragettes is not borne out by these five suffragettes, who appear eminently kissable. They are, from the left: Victoria Lidiard, suffragette, vegetarian, optician; an Indian woman studying in London and taking part in the Women's Social and Political Union's (WSPU's) Women's Coronation Procession of 1911; Christabel Pankhurst the co-founder of the movement; Annie Kenney, mill girl and a senior organizer; and Emmeline Pethick-Lawrence, the treasurer and business manager.

John Hassall (1868–1948) was a cartoonist, illustrator, painter and poster artist. After the Post Office lifted its restrictions on the design and use of postcards in 1902, the time up to the First World War was a golden age for postcards. Before 1902 postcards had to have a name and address on one side, and the message on the other. Then the Post Office allowed photographic or drawn images to appear on one side, with the message and the address on the other side.

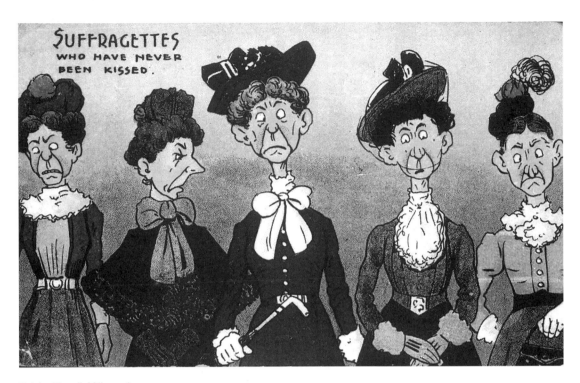

5. John Hassall, Millar and
Lang Ltd, Art Publishers,
1907.

6. *From left to right:*
Victoria Lidiard, unknown
Indian woman, Christabel
Pankhurst, Annie Kenney
and Emmeline Pethick-
Lawrence.

The Government did not give women the vote when they stuck to law-abiding methods. True to their motto 'Deeds not words', the suffragettes felt that direct action was a legitimate use of minor infringements of the law to right a major anomaly.

These drawings refer to Emmeline Pankhurst's Bill of Rights deputation to the Houses of Parliament on 29 June 1909. In an attempt to win public support for their campaign, she and eight other suffragettes tried to present a petition, claiming that it is 'the right of the subject to petition the King'. Leading the deputation from Caxton Hall, Emmeline Pankhurst was met at Strangers' Entrance by Inspectors Jarvis and Scantlebury.

This spread was published in the *Daily Mirror* and captioned 'Votes and Violence'. The newspaper did not condone the recent protest:

Many persons consider that the suffragettes are ladies with a good cause, who ought to get the vote they demand. But even sympathetic believers sometimes fail to see how a woman can prove her capacity for citizenship by showing she can effectively break a window or strike a police inspector's face.

The account 'Tale of Two Slaps' described the attack in detail:

Mr Jarvis was well known to the members of the Women's Social and Political Union as a perfectly courteous and civil officer, carrying out duties which were unpleasant to him in a courteous way . . . [Mrs Pankhurst] had read the letter from Mr Asquith's private secretary . . . and thrown it to the ground. Witness [Jarvis] then asked Mrs Pankhurst to go away, and she asked him to take a message inside the House. He declined to do so, and all the women absolutely refused to leave. Mrs Pankhurst then slapped him across the left cheek with her open hand. 'You must not do that Mrs Pankhurst,' he said, and then again asked her to leave, but she replied with a second and harder smack, and another woman took off the Inspector's cap and threw it into the roadway.

Suffragettes who had been instructed to be on hand were given the signal to 'smash up' (by Pankhurst) and government offices in Whitehall were attacked by women carrying stones wrapped in brown paper in their 'wristbags'. A hundred and eight women were arrested and charged with obstruction and malicious damage at Bow St magistrates' court the next day. The window smashers' prison sentences were from four to six weeks. Emmeline Pankhurst's case was adjourned until 9 July, and again until December when she was found guilty and fined.

This incident followed three years of escalating militancy: heckling at political meetings; campaigning against the Liberal Government at by-elections; 'pestering the politicians' as they played golf, went to church and had dinner; breaking Whitehall windows and chaining themselves to the railings at 10 Downing Street. In *Her Own Story* (1914), her autobiography, Emmeline Pankhurst explains the events of that day:

I now knew that the deputation would not be received and that the old miserable business of refusing to leave, of being forced backward, and returning again and again until arrested would have to be re-enacted. I had to take into

7. W. K. Haselden, *Daily Mirror*, 2 July 1909.

account that I was accompanied by two fragile old ladies, who, brave as they were to be there at all, could not possibly endure what I knew must quickly follow. I quickly decided that I should have to force an immediate arrest, so I committed an act of technical assault on the person of Inspector Jarvis, striking him very lightly on the cheek. He said instantly, 'I understand why you did that', and I supposed then that we would be taken. But the other police apparently did not grasp the situation, for they began pushing and jostling our women. I said to the Inspector, 'Shall I have to do it again?' and he said, 'Yes.' So I struck him lightly a second time, and then he ordered the police to make the arrests.

W. K. Haselden (1872–1953) was self-taught, working as an underwriter at Lloyd's until he went to work for the *Daily Mirror* in 1904, where he was until 1940. He also cartooned for *Punch* during that period. This series of cartoons seems to say that he has no sympathy with the suffragettes' behaviour, but his drawing of the policemen is risible. Even though the inspector is twice the size of the suffragette and the constable has a horse, neither is able to cope with this slip of a thing.

In Greek mythology Sisyphus was a King of Corinth whose punishment in Hades was to roll a heavy stone up a hill. As he reached the top, the stone rolled down again. He toiled for an eternity. It is 13 July 1910 and the artist is describing what happened in Parliament in the preceding two days. The Conciliation Committee was an all-party parliamentary committee which had been formed to draft the Conciliation Bill, a women's suffrage bill, which would be acceptable to all parties. The women's suffrage movement canvassed to persuade politicians to support the bill. The 'Antis' worked hard against it, supported by the Liberal Cabinet Ministers David Lloyd George and Winston Churchill. Yet the bill passed its second reading with a majority of over a hundred votes. But the women's suffrage movement was bitterly disappointed when Prime Minister Asquith announced he would allow the bill no further time and suspended Parliament, thereby thwarting the bill's progress until Parliament was recalled in November and making its future extremely uncertain. The women's suffrage campaigners seemed doomed to struggle like Sisyphus.

Leonard Raven-Hill's cartoon was published in *Punch*. The suffragist is strong and determined, and her burden throws a shadow over her. She is alone. The metaphor of Sisyphus is an odd one because the women's suffrage campaign was a huge group effort. Raven-Hill (1867–1942) studied at Lambeth School of Art, working for *Punch* from 1896 for forty years.

8. Leonard Raven-Hill, *Punch,* 13 July 1910.

PUNCH, OR THE LONDON CHARIVARI.—July 13, 1910.

EXCELSIOR!

Suffragist. "IT'S NO GOOD TALKING TO ME ABOUT SISYPHUS; HE WAS ONLY A MAN!"

13

Mrs Partington is a feeble figure – with no visible means of support, she is not looking up at the sunrise, so intent is she on sweeping back the tide, the terrible tide of working women, professional women and the supporters of women's suffrage. She is a Canute. She wears a daft, over-decorated hat, a silly feather boa, and her dog is a toy. She is even old-fashioned in her dress – the date of the cartoon is 1910, but her clothing is from the early nineteenth century.

Ernestine Mills (1871-1959), best known for her wonderful Arts and Crafts enamels, lampoons the opponents of votes for women. The original Mrs Partington was a by-word for stubbornly held, reactionary ideas. She is said to have tried to sweep back the ocean during the Great Storm of 1824. During the debate prior to the 1832 Reform Act (which gave the vote to half a million men, but by using the term 'male person' for the first time specifically prevented women from voting in parliamentary elections), Sidney Smith said in the House of Lords:

The Atlantic was roused. Mrs Partington's spirit was up, but I need not tell you that the contest was unequal. The Atlantic Ocean beat Mrs Partington. She was excellent at a slop or a puddle, but she should not have meddled with a tempest.

9. Ernestine Mills, published by the artist, 1910.

Raphael Tuck and Sons published the anti-suffragette card in 1912. On 27 April 1992 'The Suffragette's Vision' was realized when Betty Boothroyd became the first woman to be elected Speaker of the House of Commons. Our Madam Speaker does not wear the full-bottomed wig of her predecessors. Boothroyd is the most popular Member of Parliament: in the last four years she has been named Parliamentarian of the Year; Personality of the Year; and Communicator of the Year. Much of her time in the House of Commons is televised as a superior form of entertainment, but her command, her even-handed but firm handling of her troops, are enjoyed by many. The postcard is an unpleasant but powerful picture by an unknown artist. The Speaker seems a little like Queen Victoria, her assistant looks like an ugly bloke in drag. They are a miserable, dire warning: Betty Boothroyd is the charming reality.

10. (Below) Anon., Raphael Tuck and Sons, 1912.

11. (Below right) Betty Boothroyd, MP, Speaker of the House of Commons.

The suffragette is absent: her domain is a scene of misery and abandonment. The older child, a girl, weeps into a white cloth, her stockings have not been darned by her neglectful mother. The younger boy is slumped on the floor. The oil lamp smokes because its wick has not been trimmed. Father, the upright, hard-working man, the 'breadwinner', stands four-square and lantern-jawed to the world, returned to a scene of domestic chaos. His hands are clenched: enough is enough. His is a reactionary attitude: she acts and he reacts.

John Hassall designed this poster in 1912, for the 'Antis' – the National League for Opposing Woman Suffrage. Shattered homes was a frequent message. Men and women, often wealthy and politically highly influential, formed their own separate campaigns and organizations in 1908, amalgamating in 1910, in response to the inroads being made by the activities of the suffragettes, members of the Women's Social and Political Union. The 'Antis' were also reactionary, always reacting to the suffragettes, never acting. They met their match in the women's suffrage movement, who produced postcards and posters - lampooning them for their antediluvian ideas.

13. John Hassall, National League for Opposing Woman Suffrage, 1912.

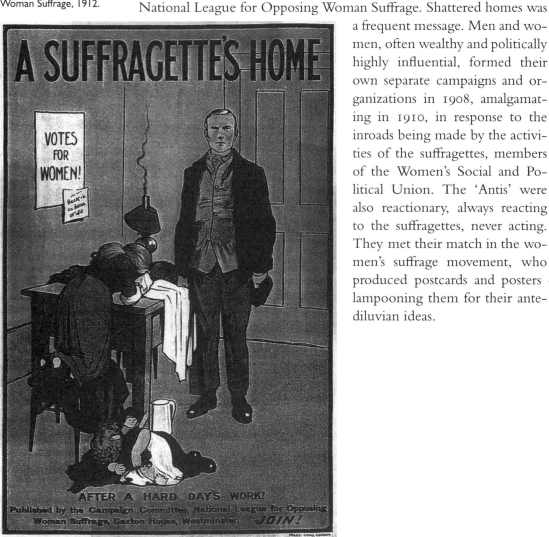

It is wartime London in 1917 and the former Prime Minister Henry Asquith is being helped aboard the suffrage omnibus by a woman conductor. (In April 1915 Glasgow Corporation employed the first women tram conductors.) Asquith had 'missed the bus' politically on several occasions before the outbreak of the First World War in 1914, and he is drawn as an elderly man who is struggling (he was sixty-five years old, and had another eleven years to live). He needs the help of this strong, young, forgiving suffragette-ish figure. The women's suffrage movement had rallied round and encouraged women to fight the war on the 'home front'.

Punch published this Bernard Partridge cartoon and an article describing Asquith's public recantation of his hostility to Women's Suffrage ... which caused a large attendance of Members, Peers and the general public ... But, after Mr Asquith's handsome admission that, by their splendid services in the War, the women had worked out their own electoral salvation, even that topic seemed to have lost most of its provocative quality; and there is a general desire to forget what the late Prime Minister described as a detestable campaign and bury the hatchet and all the other weapons employed in it.

In January 1918 the Representation of the People Act gave 8.5 million women over the age of thirty the vote.

Sir Bernard Partridge (1861–1945) cartooned for *Punch* from 1891 to 1945, becoming its Political Cartoonist in 1910. He was knighted in 1925.

14. Bernard Partridge, *Punch*, 4 April 1917.

PUNCH, OR THE LONDON CHARIVARI.—April 4, 1917.

WOMEN'S SUFFRAGE

THE CATCH OF THE SEASON.

CONDUCTORETTE (to Mr. Asquith). "COME ALONG, SIR. BETTER LATE THAN NEVER."

Women over the age of twenty-one were to be granted the vote in April 1928, putting them on equal suffrage terms with men. David Low pretends to be unnerved by a future where women may be dominant with the new Eves chucking their apple cores at a cowed Adam over the head of a mystified serpent. The Eves are from the left: Ellen Wilkinson (1891–1947), Labour MP for Middlesbrough East; novelist Rebecca West (1892–1983); Clemence Dane (1888–1965) a novelist and playwright; the writer Sheila Kaye-Smith (1887–1956) and actor Sybil Thorndyke (1882–1976).

The image is an unfunny and paranoid view of the equalization of the franchise. The tired idea of the Garden of Eden and the apple core hitting a man accidentally on the head is sub-*Beano*. An accompanying article in the *Evening Standard* describes the way the eight women Members of Parliament were often written about as objects of curiosity, even by women. 'Corrisande' in the 'Woman's World' column wrote:

15. David Low, *Evening Standard*, 18 February 1928.

Women have been in Parliament for a number of years now, but visitors still regard them as among the principal sights in the House. People sitting high

ADAM AND EVES — NEW VERSION, IN MODERN DRESS.

20

up in the Strangers' Gallery find it difficult, looking down on the assembly, to spot the women members unless they are searching specially for them. But as soon as a female voice rings out at question time everyone in the Gallery leans forward, and many rise to their feet only to be waved back by the vigilant attendants who are responsible for the observance of due parliamentary 'decorum' among the visitors.

Sir David Low (1891–1963) was born in New Zealand and moved to London in 1919. He worked for the evening newspaper the *Star*, then the *Evening Standard* in 1926. In 1950 he joined the *Daily Herald*, going to the *Manchester Guardian* in 1953. Influential and prolific, and left-wing, he had a fifty-year career and his work appeared in two hundred newspapers and magazines. He was knighted in 1962.

A Parliament made up entirely of women seemed bizarre and threatening in 1929. The way the woman on the left stretches out is still considered odd and 'unladylike'; and the same can be said about the demeanour of the woman with crossed arms. Low's cartoon reminds us that men's body language is more insolent, aggressive and self-indulgent.

At the time of the 1929 General Election there were ten women MPs in the House of Commons. Nancy, Viscountess Astor (Conservative, Plymouth Sutton) was the first to be elected in 1919. Mrs Mabel Philipson (Conservative, Berwick-upon-Tweed) followed in 1923. Also elected in 1923 was Katherine, Duchess of Atholl (Conservative, Perth and Kinross, Kinross and Western). Margaret Bondfield was the first Labour woman MP, elected for Northampton in 1923, defeated a year later, then re-elected in 1926 for Wallsend. (Bondfield would become the first woman Cabinet Minister.) Susan Lawrence followed Bondfield, first elected for East Ham North in 1923 and defeated in 1924, and re-elected in 1926 for the same constituency. Ellen Wilkinson (Labour) was elected for Middlesbrough East in 1924. Gwendolen, Countess of Iveagh (Conservative, Southend-on-Sea) became the next in 1927. Mrs Ruth Dalton was for a very brief time the Labour MP for Bishop Auckland, after what was known as a 'warming-pan election'. She joined the House in February 1929 after winning the seat at a by-election for her husband, Hugh Dalton, then Labour MP for Peckham. She handed the seat over to him later that year. Hilda Runciman also 'warmed' her husband's seat. In 1928 she became Liberal MP for St Ives, but passed her seat on to her husband Walter, who swapped his Swansea constituency for St Ives in the 1929 General Election. Jennie Lee was the last woman to join the House before the election, becoming Labour MP for Lanarkshire Northern.

16. David Low, *Evening Standard*, 1929.

THE PARLIAMENT OF THE FUTURE?

22

The enlarged female electorate was targeted by the three main political parties in the build-up to the 1929 General Election, here by the Labour Party in *Labour Woman*. The vote is the lever for a strong young woman to turn the armchair male out and over the cliff into the abyss. The artist is called 'A. Stagg' – obviously a pen-name.

Historically the Labour Party and trade union movement have been at best ambivalent about women's political rights and equal pay. The 1929 election drew on an electorate which had grown from 21.7 million in 1928 to nearly 28.85 million in 1929. The new voters were: 1.95 million women aged thirty and over, 3.29 million women aged between twenty-one and twenty-nine; and 1.9 million men aged twenty-one and over, none of whom had been enfranchised until then. Certain 'women's issues' were raised during the election. Of greatest concern were widows' pensions, followed by maternity and child welfare, the equalization of the vote, peace, the cost of living, and equal pay. The Labour Party won the election with 288 seats, the Conservatives got 260 seats, and the Liberals 59 seats.

The number of women Members of Parliament was boosted by the election. Sixty-nine women candidates stood and fifteen were successful, the Labour Party returning the largest number of new women members. New names were: Dr Ethel Bentham (Labour, Islington East); Mary Hamilton (Labour, Blackburn); Megan Lloyd George (Liberal, Anglesey); Lady Cynthia Mosley (Labour, Stoke-on-Trent); Dr Marion Phillips (Labour, Sunderland); Edith Picton-Turbeville (Labour, Shropshire, The Wrekin) and Eleanor Rathbone (Independent, Combined English Universities).

17. 'A. Stagg', *Labour Woman*, April 1929.

The Labour Woman

Edited by Dr. Marion Phillips

Vol. XVII.   No. 4

Price Twopence
Subscription with Postage
Three Shillings Annually

April, 1929

PUBLISHED BY THE LABOUR PARTY

OVER YOU GO!

PREPARING FOR VICTORY!

23

n the past there were powerful women, warriors like Boudicca (d. AD 62). For a strong woman there is a supportive man at home, or not. This one's domestic paraphernalia, his apron, pan and cloth, have made him round-shouldered, silent, weighed down. He is dressed down for the kitchen sink and she is dressed up and going to work. The *Oxford English Dictionary* defines 'career woman' as: 'one who works permanently in a profession, as opposed to one who ceases full-time work on marrying'. The terms 'career girl' and 'career woman' are used twice for the first time in 1937: once in a newspaper headline declaring 'Career Women are Different'. In 1947 the *Daily Mail* asked the question 'Should the Career Woman Make Dates?'

This cartoon was drawn by George Morrow towards the end of his long life. He was born in 1869, cartooned for *Punch* for nearly fifty years and was the art editor from 1930 to 1937. He died in 1955.

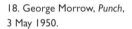

18. George Morrow, *Punch*, 3 May 1950.

'This is what comes of marrying a career woman.'

The man from Gallup Poll is quickly acquainted with Andy Capp's individualism – he is a party of one. The fact that his long-suffering wife Florrie is silent, as she often is, does not mean that she agrees with him. Usually she prefers to let him make a fool of himself. At other times she manages him or indulges him. Most often she wins 'the battle of the sexes'. Reg Smythe's working-class 'stereotypes' often break the mould, in this case by going further than the formula of voting for the same party as your husband.

Born in 1917 in Hartlepool, Reg Smythe started drawing Andy Capp for the *Daily Mirror* in 1957. Replying to a questionnaire about this cartoon, he said he believed that cartoons do not change attitudes as 'people's attitudes generally remain constant'. When asked if this drawing reflected his own attitudes, he declared: 'It's a toss-up as to who is doing the reflecting – myself or Andy Capp.'

'I'm *the party she belongs to!*'

19. Reg Smythe, *Daily Mirror*, 1958.

This is a female modern version of Hogarth's *The Rake's Progress*. She is using her sex to progress. The role of women in sex scandals has exposed the hypocrisy of male morality. The double standard was never better exposed than in the Profumo affair. A succession of women, including Oxbridge 'bluestockings', have been accused of causing havoc in high places. Their influence, personal appearance and hairstyles have become a newspaper topic. Shirley Williams, Margaret Jay, Clare Short, Glenys Kinnock, Edwina Currie and Norma Major have all been the butt of concerted attacks from the press and media. (The novels of Edwina Currie describe the cocktail of sex and politics at Westminster.)

This spread was drawn by Ronald Searle. He was born in 1920 and worked as a solicitor's clerk, then studied at Cambridge Technical College and School of Art. His cartoons were published by the *Cambridge Daily News* from 1935 to 1939 and the *Daily Express* in 1939. After the war he cartooned from 1949 to 1951 for the *Sunday Express*, and from 1949 to 1962 for *Punch*. He has published over forty books including *Ronald Searle's Non-Sexist Dictionary* in 1988. His best-loved work is about life at St Trinian's, the naughty girls' school. Searle's sexy, eccentric, arty drawings are charming and seductive.

20. Ronald Searle,
in *The Penguin Ronald Searle*,
Penguin Books, 1960.

1. Emergence

Famous at Cambridge for her affectionate nature. Rusticated. Interests herself in Social Welfare

2. Success

Outstanding success at Fabian Summer School

3. Temptation

Befriends politicians. Subscribes to Hansard. Persuaded to stand for Parliament

4. Triumph

Elected with large majority. Cancels subscription to *Mother and Home*

5. Downfall

Stamina at all-night meetings attracts ministerial attention. Under-Secretary to Minister of Defence

6. Ruin

Guest of the Week on Woman's Hour. Minister of Health. Profile in the *Lady*. D.B.E.

Edward Heath has become a male suffragette; Mrs Thatcher was the fullest heir of the suffragettes. Margaret Thatcher was detested by many because she was stern and inflexible and did not seem to be 'womanly', although she always wore skirts and carried a handbag. She is the strict mother no one wants: mothers are preferred warm and indulgent.

'The knives are out – it's a fight to the end' wrote Anthony Shrimsley, Political Editor of the *Daily Mail,* on 4 February 1975, describing Margaret Thatcher's challenge to Edward Heath for the leadership of the Conservative Party. An article by Peter Lewis was illustrated by a 'Femail' Photo Special showing the contender then, and now, and reminds us how the first woman Prime Minister, and women, were regarded and described in some circles:

Thatcher is what they have been calling her for four months now, just the name without any Mrs. It is a distinction in its way because you do not hear people talk of Castle or Williams and be quite confident that you'll know whom they mean . . . without the Barbara or the Shirley. Thatcher means a face, a bearing, a style, an image that has not changed by a hair since she entered public life in 1951 . . . Most women reach a peak of physical and intellectual confidence in their middle 30s and then slow down their personal change of style whatever the pressures of fashion. Until that time they are susceptible to change, experimenting with clothes and hairstyles and make-up until they feel they have got it right. But what is a woman to do when the traditional way for women in politics to look has been, on the whole, dowdy, unglamorous, unremarkable?

Previously women Ministers have concentrated usually on looking safe in sensible shoes. Margaret Thatcher was too good-looking to go along with that. Glamour was one of her cards . . . She hit on the combination of looking pretty but brisk, of sounding feminine but cool, of having caste but not class. She is a pioneer in her way – a symbol of her new feminine meritocracy . . . We know about that smile. Many have been struck by that smile. At full intensity . . . it is dazzling . . . It is the smile of a woman who wants to be thought of as capable. And also to be thought equal . . . Since she has had her share of abuse, possibly rather more than her share because a woman is an emotional symbol, especially considered with another emotional symbol such as milk and larders. But the abuse broke like water on a rock . . . [As Minister of Education she stopped free school milk, and often told how she kept plenty of tinned food in her larder in case of shortages.] The rock was not washed away . . .

The results of the contest were announced the next day: Thatcher 130 votes; Heath 119 votes and Hugh Fraser 16 votes. Anthony Shrimsley described her victory as having 'smashed taboos to capture the Tory leadership and make history'.

'Mac' (Stanley McMurtry) was born in Edinburgh in 1936. He studied at Birmingham College of Art and worked in animation before joining the *Daily Sketch* as Political and Social Cartoonist in 1969. He joined the *Daily Mail* in 1971. He has been influenced by Ronald Searle, Giles, Bill Tidy and Gary Larson. Although 'Mac' does not think that cartoons can change anything, he believes that they can

prick pomposity, lighten an otherwise dreary subject and make people think. In this case the goal was to make people laugh, not to change their attitudes. My attitude is that women and men should be treated equally at all times and rise or fall to positions of great power only because of their talents and not because of their sex.

He hopes his work has developed a lot:

I look back at the work I did when I first started and wonder how I ever got started. It was terrible. I hope in a few years' time to look back on the work I'm doing now and consider it terrible. Once an artist or cartoonist starts to be pleased with his work then he will never improve.

21. 'Mac' (Stanley McMurtry), *Daily Mail*, 4 February 1975.

'Constable, would you mind removing that suffragette from the railings?'

Nicholas Garland has dropped Mrs Thatcher's frilly drawers to make the point that defence cuts weaken and could leave her open to 'invasion'. (The defence budget has been cut steadily over the past thirty years.) Mrs Thatcher became Britain's first woman Prime Minister when the Conservative Party won the 1979 General Election, serving eleven and a half years in the job. In 1976 the Russians called her 'The Iron Lady', a name she apparently revelled in. In April 1982 Britain went to war with Argentina after the invasion of the Falkland Islands.

Nicholas Garland was born in 1935 and studied at the Slade School of Fine Art from 1954 to 1957. From 1966 to 1986 he was the *Daily Telegraph*'s Political Cartoonist. After five years at the *Independent*, from 1986 to 1991 he returned to the *Daily Telegraph*. His work is also published in the *Spectator*. Garland describes the origination of 'The Iron Lady?', which he drew for the *Daily Telegraph* but which was published in the *Spectator*:

22. Nicholas Garland, *Spectator*, 1 November 1980.

THE IRON LADY?

My job is to do a daily cartoon, this one was just the next day's one. (Incidentally the editor [Bill Deedes] turned it down with the words 'If you think I'm going to publish a drawing of the Prime Minister with her knickers down you are out of your mind' or words to that effect. I would like to make it clear that he was laughing while he spoke. I did another cartoon and published this particular drawing in the *Spectator*.)

Garland does not think that cartoons change anything

except in the sense that they play a modest part, or may do, in very generalized opinion forming. Cartoons tend to reflect attitudes that are already widely held ... There is frequently a clash between politicians' rhetoric and their actions. In this case 'The Iron Lady?' contemplating defence cuts was an example of such a clash.

He has been influenced 'by many cartoonists, above all by 'Vicky'. Lately I have been studying the caricatures of Richard Winnington and have also been influenced by Steve Bell.'

People think in clichés and mouth clichés. Women who aspire to power on any level are more frequently the butt of negative adjectives than men. Helena Normanton became the first woman barrister in 1921; Margaret Bondfield, the first woman Cabinet Minister in 1929; Anne Loughlin was the first woman President of the Trades Union Congress in 1943; Helena Normanton and Rose Heilbron were the first two women King's Counsellors in 1949; Dame Barbara Salt, the first woman ambassador (to Israel) in 1962; Dame Elizabeth Lane became the first woman High Court Judge in 1965; Margaret Thatcher, the first woman leader of a political party in Britain and the first woman Prime Minister in 1975 and 1979 respectively; Baroness Young was the first woman Leader of the House of Lords in 1981; Mary Donaldson became the first woman Lord Mayor of London in 1983; and Betty Boothroyd, MP, became the first woman Speaker of the House of Commons in 1992.

Viv Quillin was born in 1946. She left school at sixteen, trained as a graphic designer at twenty-eight and has been a cartoonist ever since. She started drawing cartoons when she was at school.

[My headmistress] sent my sketch book to a cartoonist, who said, 'Don't try to make a living out of it.' At college I was told I would never earn a living . . . In fact, I've supported myself and three children with varying degrees of affluence until they all grew up and left home.

23. Viv Quillin, in *Women's Work*, Hamish Hamilton, 1984.

GLOSSARY OF TERMS IN COMMON USE

Quillin thinks that cartoons change things because 'creating the cartoon clarifies my thoughts and feelings, so that I can talk and think without confusion'. For her this image is 'one of those "Aha" jokes which help you lay your finger on the dynamics of a situation and you say, "Aha that's exactly how it is. "' It also shows 'the way I think that most people (including myself) see me and other women'.

Committees are sources of power and give validity to actions. Women are still under-represented everywhere. By exaggerating this and showing no women on a women's rights committee, this cartoon reminds us that in a righteous world there would be about 50 per cent of women on every committee, bench, executive, and so on.

Nick Hobart was born in London in 1939. Blitz damage forced his family to move several times, but he survived to attend Dulwich College, and then Purbrook Grammar School near Portsmouth. Before he emigrated to Canada in 1972, he worked as a school teacher and as a building society clerk. He now lives in Florida, where, he says, '75 per cent of cartoon editors are women, thank heavens'. He came up with this cartoon when he was 'musing on (then) current events'. He has been influenced by, among others, Searle, Starke, Price, Fougasse and Collins. He says this drawing took him thirty minutes to complete.

24. Nick Hobart, *Punch*, 18 March 1988.

'The committee on women's rights
will now come to order.'

All visual codes, which include the current styles of women's shoes, have meaning. Part of the purpose of this book is to unravel the meanings that are encoded in drawings. Fashions somehow mirror the age – the radical trainer can become the working-class sign, the fetishistic heel can become merely fashionable. Signs change in meaning, and whatever you wear places you somewhere.

This is a densely packed and superbly knowing cartoon depicting the history and 'progress' of feminism as told by the size and sound of the heel of women's shoes.

Posy Simmonds was born in 1945. She studied fine art and French at the Sorbonne in Paris and graphics at the Central School of Art and Design.

[I have looked at cartoons] ever since I could read, I loved comics – *Beano*, *Superman* . . . and I loved old bound volumes of *Punch*, particularly 1840–1900, its impenetrable jokes and captions like short plays. I like Charles Keene, Du Maurier, Phil May and John Leech. I also admired Ronald Searle, Pont, Giles, Saul Steinberg, Ungerer, Siné . . . Hogarth, Rowlandson, Gillray and Daumier.

It takes Simmonds three days to produce an image like this: a day to think; a day to write; and a day to draw. She does not feel that cartoons change things, more that they 'create awareness, provide recognition and an economical form for critical ideas. They can ridicule, embarrass . . . they can also reassure.'

25. Posy Simmonds,
Guardian, 1989.

The poster referred to in this cartoon is on page 17. This strip is about continuity and the lack of change. Amber the TV producer and Doris the cleaner talk about the suffragette poster and compare it to the situation in South Africa. Doris compares it to her own situation. Amber sees the poster as a job opportunity, as this book is to its author, and the cartoon was to Ros Asquith. Reader, compare this situation to your own.

Ros Asquith first became interested in cartooning through the work of Giles, James Thurber, Ronald Searle, Posy Simmonds, Steve Bell and the *New Yorker* cartoonists. She went to Camberwell School of Art. *Doris* runs weekly in the *Guardian*. Doris 'comments on the vagaries of the chattering classes. They talk, she *thinks*.' Asquith says she satirizes herself – she is both Amber and Doris.

26. Ros Asquith, *Guardian*,
10 March 1990.

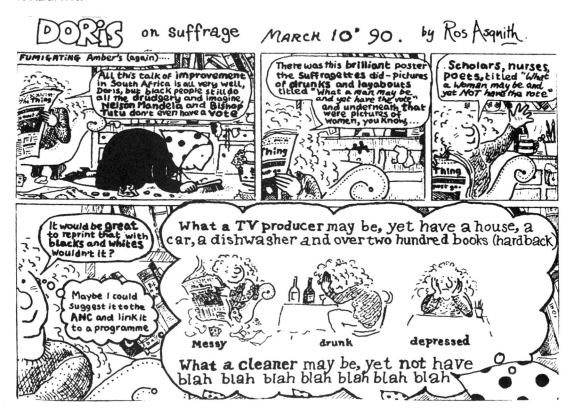

The 'Antis', the Edwardian opponents of the women's suffrage campaign, are reborn in this bizarre genuine organization. The five men at the front are unappealingly masculine: they are bald and five o'clock shadowed. Their body language tells us they are masculine men. There are men and women who subscribe to the views expressed by this organization: Neil Lyndon and Camille Paglia, the 'power feminist', are probably the best known.

Grizelda Grislingham was born in London in 1966. She started to study fine art but left after two terms to read English and drama at Hull University. Her cartoons have been published in various magazines and newspapers, including *Diva*, *London Cyclist* and the *Pink Paper*. She drew this cartoon 'on spec'. 'The idea came as soon as I heard of the organization. It seemed obvious that it would have been set up by men ... I still think it's a ludicrous and insulting organization, and can't believe it really exists,' she says. She thinks that cartooning does change things:

It influences and comments upon contemporary attitudes in the same way as other media, TV, film, fiction and journalism ... Cartoons that make feminist statements may only confirm what a feminist believes anyway, but they might also offer a new perception of an old idea.

27. Grizelda Grislingham, Cath Tate Cards, 1992.

This 'New Man' is an old masher underneath. After the Labour Party's defeat in 1992, Barbara Follett founded Emily's List UK, which raises money to help women trying to be selected as Labour Party candidates. They receive £1,000 towards administrative costs and training. The acronym: Early Money Is Like Yeast (it makes dough rise), and the idea are borrowed from the United States. (In 1995 Barbara Follett was selected as the prospective Labour Party candidate to fight the Stevenage seat at the next General Election.)

'Millennium Basin' is the work of Kate Charlesworth. She was born in 1950, in Barnsley, Yorkshire, of a 'mixed marriage':

[My parents were] working class and lower middle class. Dad was a self-employed baker, Ma managed the shop and I read and drew a lot. Grandad was the archetypal Yorkshire miner: flat cap, white silk scarf, whippet. And he bred canaries. Grandma didn't say much ... At some point (I don't know when) the idea of becoming a cartoonist occurred to me. I read the *Beano*, and remember being impressed by the artwork for the Bash Street Kids, Minnie the Minx ... much later I realized these were all drawn by the great Leo Baxendale. As my parents took the *Express*, I saw Giles and Osbert Lancaster (from whom I learnt it was OK to write long captions); I discovered Ronald Searle and St Trinian's ... At thirteen I discovered DC Comics – no other brand was acceptable – and I liked Thomas Henry's 'William' illustrations very much.

Despite the evidence, cartooning hasn't been seen as 'something women do'. Although if, when I'm asked what I do, the answer's always greeted with surprise, and it's often difficult to know whether this is because of the unusual nature of the job, or my gender, or both. When I first began drawing cartoons, I came to a decision that I would never sign a piece of artwork with my surname alone; I thought it was important that women cartoonists should be visible ... My cartoons, especially 'Millennium Basin' ... tend to focus on anxiety, pretension, frustration, insecurity, the things that make life worth living. It's basically about people behaving like pillocks.

28. Kate Charlesworth,
Guardian, 6 January 1996.

2 | Work

It used to be said that a woman's place is in the home: now there is a place for women everywhere, because women have fought to be accepted at the ballot-box, at work and in education. The First World War, the first industrialized war, used so many men as cannon-fodder that it needed many women in the factories to replace them and provide them with armaments. Women also worked at other male jobs in transport and the Civil Service, and at traditionally female jobs like nursing. After the Great War nothing could be the same again. Social changes, such as the emergence of housing catering specifically for working single women, the mass-production of clothes and the increase of public transport in the big cities, freed women to determine their careers to some extent. Many were shop-girls, typists, clerks and factory workers. Domestic service, a huge industry for women in the nineteenth century, along with farming, was ending, it disappeared completely after 1945.

In the Second World War many women were 'Wrens' (WRNS, Women's Royal Naval Service), 'Waafs' (WAAF, Women's Auxiliary Air Force), 'Waacs' (WAAC, Women's Army Auxiliary Corps), Land Girls, and so on. Many women with children were on their own and, since the war was fought in some distant theatres – North Africa, Italy and Greece, the Far East – remained lone parents for several years. These social upheavals, like those brought about by the new technology of the telephone, the typewriter, the conveyor belt and the sewing machine, caused considerable change in woman's role. There was increased responsibility, power and learning on the one hand; and wage slavery and exploitation on the other hand.

Some of our cartoonists saw these changes as mere role reversal, with women rather than men in positions of power. In fact, men continued to run the show – they just needed women to do more things, as well as bring up children.

After the Second World War, with equal education for all, and the universities gradually benefiting from the 1944 Education Act (which raised the school-leaving age to fifteen and provided free secondary education for all, dividing schools into grammar, technical and secondary modern schools), some women began to achieve their potential and ambitions. Yet today women can see the 'glass ceiling', bang their heads on it, but they cannot break it. Some men's inability to cope with the presence of women in the workplace is demonstrated in sexist language and sexual harassment. Women have shown in the classroom and the boardroom that they are at least the equal of men: it is economic sense, at the least, to give them an equal chance to shine.

Britain is at war, the Great War of 1914–18, and women are needed as 'ministering angels', that is, nurses. So serious was the emergency that the moderate and militant women's suffrage organizations called off their campaigns and encouraged women to help fight the war on the 'home front'. Millicent Garrett Fawcett said: 'Let us prove ourselves worthy of citizenship, whether our claim be recognized or not.' Patriotism, and in the case of many of the suffragettes, jingoism, was the rhetoric during the war years. (Only women like Sylvia Pankhurst, Emmeline Pankhurst's younger daughter, who was a pacifist and socialist, continued to fight for the vote and

29. 'A. Patriot' (Alfred Pearse), *Votes For Women*, 14 August 1914.

VOTES FOR WOMEN

EDITED BY FREDERICK AND EMMELINE PETHICK LAWRENCE

VOL. VII. (New Series), No. 336.   FRIDAY, AUGUST 14, 1914.   Price 1d. Weekly (Post Free 1½d.)

WOMEN TO THE RESCUE!

A. Patriot

Oh, it's woman this, and woman that, and "Woman cannot fight!"
But it's "Ministering Angel!" when the wounded come in sight.

denounced women's involvement in the war.) On 10 August, six days after the declaration of war with Germany, the Government released all suffragette prisoners on the understanding that they suspend their militant activities. What the suffrage movement had said about women's abilities in the campaign was exemplified by what they did between 1914 and 1918.

'Keep the Home Fires Burning' was a song written by Ivor Novello during the First World War. Women took over jobs previously done by men, with the exception of underground coal-mining and some work in munitions. As well as nursing, they were grave-diggers, window-cleaners, chimney sweeps, car mechanics, policewomen, lorry drivers, postwomen, guards on the London Underground, aeroplane mechanics, coal heavers, tram and bus conductors, carpenters, bricklayers and workers in the chemical industries. One and a half million more women were at work in 1918 than in 1914. For example, in the metal industries the number of women rose from 170,000 in 1914 to 594,000 in 1918; and in chemicals the figures are 40,000 in 1914 and 104,000 in 1918. In transport there were 18,200 women employed in 1914, and by 1918 their numbers had risen to 117,200.

Alfred Pearse (1856–1933), also known as 'A Patriot', designed several posters for the suffragettes, and had produced a weekly cartoon for the front page of *Votes For Women* since 1909. He was a wood engraver and book illustrator. The *Illustrated London News*, *Punch*, *Strand Magazine* and *Boy's Own Paper* published his drawings. Laurence Housman (1865–1959), whose poem 'Oh, it's woman this, and woman that' is quoted in the caption, was also a critic and illustrator, and a founder member of the Suffrage Atelier. In the early 1890s he had been a leading book illustrator; in 1895 he was the art critic of the *Manchester Guardian*.

Role reversal: unusually for the times, and indeed now, she is the boss and he is the secretary. In the early days of the revolution in office technology, 'typewriter' was the name given to the person who used the machine, not to the machine itself. Nowadays the young woman would be accused of of sexual harassment. She is a 'fast girl' smoking her cigarette in a confident, even 'mannish', way. She is not only the boss but the sexual predator, and he is subservient and the sexual object. He does not look very sexy.

Wallis Mills (1878–1940) drew for *Punch* from 1905 to 1939.

30. Wallis Mills, *Punch*,
21 January 1931.

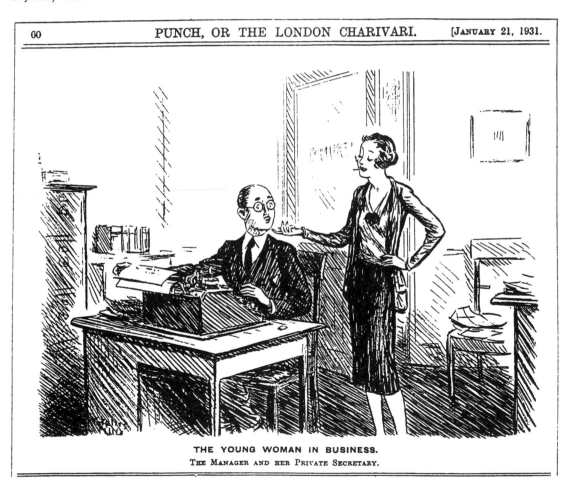

THE YOUNG WOMAN IN BUSINESS.
THE MANAGER AND HER PRIVATE SECRETARY.

45

A romantic moment in wartime Britain, as a woman welder is being wooed by a male colleague. She has halted work for a moment – we do not know her reaction because she is veiled. Because of her protective clothing she appears to be a huge de-feminized monster, but he is wooing her with flowers. This is a cartoon of contrasts – between love and work; male and female; the foundry and flowers – and opposites – she is huge, he is tiny; she is powerful, he is the supplicant; she is up and he is down.

The author of this book cover, cartoonist Giles, was also an animator and journalist. Carl Ronald Giles was born in London in 1916. During the Second World War he cartooned for *Reynolds News*, the *Daily Mail* and the *Sunday Express*. In 1959 he was awarded the OBE. He died in 1995.

32. Carl Ronald Giles, cover of *Laughs with the Workers*, compiled and printed by S. Evelyn Thomas, 1943.

I t is 1943, and married and single women have volunteered, or been conscripted, to do work usually done by men who are away at the war. Our heroine is able to do only part-time housework because she is working in a factory, perhaps in munitions, and being a housewife is now no longer a restriction but a part-time job.

Although the work was hard, often monotonous and sometimes dangerous, wages in factories were higher than in the pre-war years, and male workers in 'registered occupations', who had not been called up for active service, could be resentful and obstructive. But many women enjoyed their improved earnings, freedom and independence, and found the work fulfilling. Women's job opportunities, particularly in the electrical trades and light engineering, were broadened in the post-war period. By 1951 22 per cent of married women had jobs, much of it part-time work, compared to 10 per cent before 1939.

33. William Augustus
Sillince, *Punch*, 9 June 1943.

'I'm not here all day – I have to go and do part-time housework.'

49

The National Service Act was passed in 1941, compelling women between the ages of eighteen and fifty to register for war work. Only elderly women or those with young children and husbands at home were exempt. The Government could direct women to any job where the need was greatest. The Act was so successful that it was suspended at the end of 1944: by 1943 there were 1.5 million more women at work in these key industries than in 1939. By the end of the war some 2 million women were engaged in war work of one kind or another.

Born in London in 1906, the cartoonist William Augustus Sillince was also a painter and a writer. His faces and figures are expressive and cheeky against the seemingly loud and dirty factory. His lines and marks suit the subject. After studying at the Central School of Arts and Crafts, he worked in advertising. He contributed cartoons for *Punch* for nearly forty years, from 1938 to 1974, the year he died.

rsula has said, 'We can get it from that little woman round the corner.' Quartermasters in the army were often grocers in civilian life. The uniforms make Ursula and her superior officer look even more feminine; in their tightly buttoned clothing their curves are exaggerated.

Osbert Lancaster (1908–86) was a writer, theatre designer and painter as well as a cartoonist. His career with the *Daily Express* spanned the Forties, Fifties, Sixties and Seventies. In 1953 he was awarded a CBE and in 1957 he was knighted.

34. Osbert Lancaster, in *More Pocket Cartoons*, John Murray, 1943.

" And another thing, Ursula—in this regiment we do not refer to the Quartermaster-Sergeant as ' the little woman round the corner ' ! "

Nursing goes on at all hours and is a very responsible job. It is 1947, two years after the end of the war, and women still step into 'masculine' roles. The contrast in this drawing is strong: she is vibrant, youthful and energetic – he is a stiff, middle-aged civil servant; she is powerful and wields a pick-axe – he wields an umbrella; she is bare-armed and muscular – he wears a suit and tie and handkerchief. It is good to praise the nurses' strength without showing a nurse.

'NEB' (Ronald Niebour) cartooned for the *Oxford Mail* until he joined the *Daily Mail*, in 1938, where he stayed until 1960.

35. 'NEB' (Ronald Niebour),
Daily Mail, 12 September
1947.

"I started training to become a
nurse—but the work was too ex-
hausting." —*by NEB.*

The first Royal Tournament was held at the Agricultural Hall, Islington, in 1880. (It was originally titled 'The Grand Military Tournament and Assault-at-Arms'.) In 1947 the Tournament moved to Earl's Court.

The Royal Tournament is still an advertisement and recruiting opportunity for the armed forces. In this drawing the uniforms are based on military fashions of the past, when dashing young 'blades' dressed in an extravagant manner. Fashionable but not practical. Arthur Horner's cartoon points out the absurdity of the men's hostile reaction to women competitors, who made their début in the 1947 Tournament. The woman depicted looks more masculine than the men.

Arthur Horner (1916–1997) was born in Melbourne, Australia, and studied at East Sydney Technical School. His earliest cartoons were published by the *Sydney Bulletin*. In 1946 he moved to London to study at the Central School of Arts and Crafts. In the Fifties his work appeared in the *News Chronicle*, in the Sixties it was published in the *Guardian* and *Daily Mail*. Between 1966 and 1971 he was the Political Cartoonist of the *New Statesman*. In 1976 he returned to Australia.

36. Arthur Horner, *News Chronicle*, 8 June 1951.

HORNER VISITS THE ROYAL TOURNAMENT

" Dammit, now they're letting women in, the Tournament will become just a fashion parade ! "

t is 1954 and the equal pay issue is to the fore, again. When this cartoon was published in the *Daily Mirror* the Chancellor of the Exchequer was R. A. Butler, who served from 1951 to 1956. He had succeeded Hugh Gaitskell, the Labour Chancellor from 1950 to 1951. 'Butskellism' was a term used to describe a party consensus (after 1945) on progressive social policies and the maintenance of a mixed economy with private and public sectors. The best efforts of Margaret Thatcher ensured that 'Butskellism' is now almost redundant.

In 1955 equal pay was agreed for teachers, civil servants and local government officers. In 1970 the Equal Pay Act stipulated that equal pay for men and women doing the same job had to be brought in within five years. The Equal Value Amendment to the Equal Pay Act, passed in 1984, allowed women to claim equal pay to men doing similar but different jobs, if they were considered to be of equal value. Forty years on from 'Vicky''s drawing, women in some jobs still strive to get pay equal to that of their male colleagues.

'Vicky' (Victor Weisz) was born in Berlin in 1913, escaping from the Nazis and settling in Britain in 1935. His work was published in the *Evening Standard*, the *Daily Mail* and the *Daily Telegraph*, before he joined the *Daily Mirror* in 1954, and then rejoined the *Evening Standard* in 1958. He committed suicide in 1966.

37. 'Vicky' (Victor Weisz), *Daily Mirror*, 9 March 1954.

Spoken at a cocktail party in 1972, with the memory of Hiroshima and Nagasaki only a generation away, her reply reminds us of the CND and the Aldermaston Marches. The Campaign for Nuclear Disarmament was founded in 1958: the first secretary, Peggy Duff, remembered the unveiling of the banner in her autobiography *Left, Left, Left* (1971):

He [Gerald Hopton, designer of the symbol] unrolled . . . a long strip of black cloth. He attached a bamboo pole to each end and requisitioned two people to hold them. The strip was about six yards long and it was designed to be carried sideways along the side of a march by two people on foot or on bicycles. On the back cloth were the words 'Nuclear Disarmament' in white and at

38. 'Michael ffolkes' (Brian Davis), *Punch*, 2 August 1972.

'*And* **why** *are there no women nuclear physicists? Because women believe in Life,* **that's** *why there are no women nuclear physicists.*'

each end the strange symbol in white against the black: the broken cross inside the circle. He told us what the symbol meant. First, the semaphore for the initials, ND. Second, the broken cross means the death of man, the circle was the unborn child. It represented the threat of death by nuclear weapons to all mankind, and, because this was new, the threat to the unborn child. He 'sold' us the symbol that night – and not only the symbol, but also, for a long time, the colours too, the white on black or the black on white, which was part of the symbolism. Stark and funereal.

By 1960 CND had 459 local groups and brought 60,000 to meetings in Trafalgar Square. A lot of women were CND activists in the Fifties and Sixties. The Seventies were the decade of the Women's Liberation Movement, when women struggled in a wide variety of single-issue campaigns, not only for peace, but, for instance, in community politics and anti-Vietnam War protests. In the summer of 1981 women set off from Cardiff to Greenham Common aerodrome, where missiles were stored, on a 'walk for life', to protest at the prospect of mass nuclear destruction. They copied the suffragettes' tactic of chaining themselves to the railings, in their case the perimeter fence of the base, and demonstrated the kind of courage, in their daring and dangerous campaign, which their Edwardian predecessors would have recognized, and of which they would have been proud.

Lise Meitner (1878–1968) is the only woman physicist listed in the *Biographical Dictionary of Physicists* (1984). An Austrian-born Swedish physicist, she was one of the first scientists to study radioactive decay. Her most famous work was done in 1938, describing for the first time the splitting of uranium under neutron bombardment. During the Second World War she was invited to participate in the nuclear bomb programme but refused, hoping that such a weapon would not be feasible. The *Dictionary* concludes: 'Meitner was a distinguished scientist who made important contributions to nuclear physics despite having to overcome both sexual and racial discrimination.'

'Michael ffolkes' (Brian Davis) was born in 1925 and studied at St Martin's School of Art from 1941 to 1943 and at Chelsea School of Art from 1946 to 1949. *Punch* started to publish his work regularly from 1946. His cartoons have appeared in the *New Yorker*, the *Daily Telegraph*, *Private Eye*, *Playboy* and the *Sunday Telegraph*. *Punch* published this cartoon as part of a spread titled 'Eternally ffeminine'. 'ffolkes' died in 1988.

In this Cath Jackson cartoon the man hectors the overworked and underpaid 'skivvy' for her lack of gratitude. In 1980 4 out of every 5 part-timers were female: 40 per cent of female workers work part-time. Such women have to juggle two jobs, work and housework, and their choices of work are narrower than women in full-time employment. Other workers and trade union members sometimes see them as a threat to job security. Part-timers find it difficult to be active members of a trade union. A 1979 European Economic Community sample survey found that the United Kingdom had 39 per cent of women in the total workforce and at 41 per cent, the highest percentage of female part-timers. In West Germany the figures were 38 per cent and 28 per cent respectively; in the Netherlands 25 per cent and 28 per cent; in France 38 per cent and 18 per cent, and in Italy 29 per cent and 17 per cent.

Cath Jackson was born in 1957.

39. Cath Jackson, in *Part-time Workers Need Full-time Rights*, Ann Sedley, National Council for Civil Liberties (now known as Liberty), 1980.

The Sex Discrimination Act (1975) made discrimination between men and women unlawful in employment, education, training and the provision of housing, goods, facilities and services. Discriminatory advertisements were also made illegal. Treating a person less favourably than another on the grounds of his or her sex is regarded as sex discrimination. The Equal Opportunities Commission was established to assist the enforcement of both this and the Equal Pay Act (1970).

The man reads the newspaper, the woman is a modern-day hunter-gatherer of food, demonstrating her eligibility for the physically demanding job of bricklaying. There is a sexual division of labour, his calling is to read the, often male, news-stories. It is a bitty and impressionistic line, which leaves the reader to fill in movement and detail: it is convincing.

Jo Harvatt was born in 1957 and lives in London. She describes herself as an 'ex-solicitor and sometimes cartoonist'. She has just graduated with a BA in Fine Art and Illustration and is now 'starving in a garret'. She says that the idea for this cartoon came primarily from her mother, 'a deceptively sweet-looking, white-haired little old lady'.

40. Jo Harvatt, in *Women Draw 1984: Sixty-six Cartoonists Eye the Present and the Future*, The Women's Press, 1984.

58

This is a circular argument like G. C. Lichtenberg's 'How convenient it is that cats have two holes in their fur just where their eyes are'. God has been used to justify many things: the Spanish Inquisition; the First World War; the domestic ideology of the two spheres: the public world for men and the private world for women. This is a simple, elegant drawing where body language echoes the text. His posture is barking and hers is expectant, hoping and waiting to hear something revealing.

The first woman banker and the first chartered accountant were appointed in 1910; Charity Taylor was the first woman prison governor in 1945; Monica Milne, the first woman diplomat in 1946; the first woman bank manager was Hilda Harding in 1958. The Stock Exchange did not allow women to join until 1973.

Cartoonist Viv Quillin says:

As a girl I didn't know of any women cartoonists (no Posy in those days). I admired and emulated Ronald Searle's spiky pen lines and beautiful subtle colours. And his bizarre optical jokes. Much later I got hold of Nicole Hollander's American cartoon strip on Sylvia, the tough middle-aged Jewish single mother, and wished I could be the producer of great strips. The *Sourcream* women cartoonists collective, which I was part of, helped enormously by affirming each other's work. This was fifteen years ago, when aggression towards feminism was much more overt than it is now, and I felt like a lone voice shouting in the dark a lot of the time. I love Angela Martin's simplicity and brilliant expressions.

41. Viv Quillin, in *Women Draw 1984: Sixty-six Cartoonists Eye the Present and the Future,* The Women's Press, 1984.

If God had intended women to think he'd have given them better jobs

The poor conditions of work endured by many women are illustrated here. This woman's job is to be a toy. She is decorative, rarely used – it is an annual job. She is pretty but out of reach. The uselessness of keeping the dress is the parting shot. There is a contrast between the traditional beauty of the fairy and the slumped, moaning misery of the worker who has downed tools, crossed her legs and folded her arms. If the subject were a man he would be Father Christmas.

This Angela Martin cartoon was one of a series of alternative Christmas cards originally produced for Dale Spender and Pandora Press. 'Women and Turkeys Against Christmas', 'The Matriarchy Strike Back' and 'Three Wise Men: Are You Serious?' are also included in the series. 'Part-time Fairy' has since been published by the Women's Press and Leeds Postcards. Martin was inspired by her sister who worked for an airline, her own involvement in feminist campaigns in Manchester and the trade union courses she had taken between 1982 and 1993, when she drew this cartoon. Born in 1952, she studied textiles and fashion at Middlesex Polytechnic, and then got an MA in Textile History from Winchester School of Art. Influenced by Claire Brétecher, Mel Calman, Seventies feminist cartoonists and Gary Larson, Martin thinks that cartoons 'can make someone see something in a different way' and that they 'can reassure and sometimes challenge the "converted" and the opposition, and can make people think and laugh'.

42. Angela Martin, Leeds Postcards, 1984.

The boss treats the long-suffering Miss Wallis as 'one of the chaps', as if she has lost her femininity. He is asking 'a man of the world' what sexist remarks are like but his question actually is a sexist remark, because 'he' is a woman.

Riana Duncan is a cartoonist, illustrator and writer. Born in Paisley in 1950, she studied at the Free Academy of Fine Arts in The Hague. The *Guardian*, *Punch*, *Men Only*, the *Spectator* and the *Observer* have published her drawings.

43. Riana Duncan, *Punch*, 28 August 1985.

'You're a man of the world, Miss Wallis. Tell me, what are sexist remarks really like?'

n the discussion on changing gender roles, references to role reversals are often made. There are occasions in our culture when women have a 'hen night', or there is a 'strippergram'.

Posy Simmonds says: '"The World turned Upside-down" was certainly the most popular strip – from the number of prints *Guardian* readers asked for and the requests for reproduction from media (TV), books, magazines, Open University and students doing their theses.'

44. Posy Simmonds,
Guardian, 1987.

45. (Right) ('The woman goes out of the house . . .) Attributed to Martin Engelbrecht, *c.*1750, *The Topsy-Turvy World* exhibition catalogue, Goethe Institute, London, 1985.

46. (Below) ('The Upside-down World') A. Scala, *c.* 1810, *The Topsy-Turvy World* exhibition catalogue, Goethe Institute, London, 1985.

iana Duncan's cartoon is about men's appropriation of women's ideas and work. Rosalind Franklin died in 1958, aged thirty-seven, having received no acknowledgement of her role in the discovery in 1952 of the double helix found in DNA. Her research was shown by colleague Maurice Wilkins, allegedly without her knowledge or permission, to James Watson and Francis Crick. This enabled them to formulate a new model which demonstrated the double helix, thus guaranteeing them a place in history: in 1962 Watson, Crick and Wilkins were awarded Nobel Prizes for their work on the structure of DNA.

47. Riana Duncan, *Punch*,
8 January 1988.

'*That's an excellent suggestion, Miss Triggs. Perhaps one of the men here would like to make it.*'

ate Charlesworth drew this cartoon spread for *All That . . . The Other Half of History* (1986) a playful women's history resource book. Some of the other jobs included in the book are: priestess, media person, pit-brow lass, prostitute, devoted companion, bargee, needlewoman and knocker-up.

Charlesworth has been influenced by cartoonists like 'Anton', Posy Simmonds, Nicole Hollander, Claire Brétecher, Alison Bechdel, Carolyn Risdale and Julie Doucet. She says:

48. Kate Charlesworth, in *All That ... The Other Half of History*, Kate Charlesworth and Marsaili Cameron, Pandora Books, 1986.

I'd be pleased if I thought anything in my drawings had helped someone to consider another way of being, or another way of approaching issues, in a more positive light, particularly if they'd previously viewed the subject from a position of hostility. [I use a] Gillott's 404 drawing nib, Leonard's 506 for lettering, Faber-Castell pencils, W&N Series 7 'o' brush, Rotring ink, masking fluid, Bockingford 90 'not' paper, and too much process white and Pentel correct.

Equality is an all-purpose word expressing an idea with which we all agree, but it can mean anything; it is broad and vague. As Victor Hugo said, everyone is free to sleep under the bridges of Paris, or stay at the Ritz. 'Equal' does not mean 'the same as'. Women have equal rights with men but they have different needs, and there can be no equality at work without paid maternity leave. The boss man has a would-be seductive and quizzical gaze. His pen is his symbol of power, as is his old school tie. He is not really asking the question, he is telling his female interlocutor she can have one or the other, not both.

Jacky Fleming was born in 1955 and went to the North London Collegiate School, according to her a 'suffragette school'. From there she did a Foundation year at Chelsea School of Art, and then went on to the University of Leeds. She admires Brétecher's work and technique, Paula Rego's etchings and Frida Kahlo's courage. She says her own cartoons are 'about what it is like to be female in a man's world. I try to see the general in the particular, and find the essence of the generality, not the received version of it.' She uses her 'grandfather's marbled dip-pen holders and the nibs he kept in beautiful little boxes'.

49. Jacky Fleming, in *Be a Bloody Train Driver*, Penguin Books, 1991.

oris and Amber have a long and begrudging history together. Doris is in the bind of having to wait for the rest of her wages until the next week. She is beholden to Amber who is far better paid than she is. Class pervades this cartoon, a wine label versus a fiver.

Ros Asquith says that her cartoons are about 'mainly recognition humour', and that 'possibly the humour of women and men is different, which might account for the otherwise surprising lack of women cartoonists in the mainstream, since editors of the national newspapers are overwhelmingly male'. She uses Rapidoliner pens.

50. Ros Asquith, *Guardian*,
24 October 1992.

n the 1993 autumn Budget Kenneth Clarke, the Chancellor of the Exchequer, announced that the age for a retirement pension would be made equal for men and women at sixty-five, phased in between the years 2010 and 2020. Women who were under the age of forty-four at the time of the announcement will be affected, having to wait until they are sixty-five to collect their state pension.

'Matt' (Matthew Pritchett) drew this cartoon, which appeared on the front page of the *Daily Telegraph*. He was born in 1965 and studied graphics at St Martin's School of Art. His work uses the language of 'cattiness' about a woman's age extended to cover the state pension. He has worked for the *Daily Telegraph* since 1988, and says he 'cartoons to make people laugh, not to change their attitudes'. Influenced by cartoons in the *New Yorker*, his style 'has not changed radically over the years . . . I hope [my cartoons] get better.'

'She claims she's worried about the new retirement age but I happen to know she's too old to be affected'

51. 'Matt' (Matthew Pritchett), *Daily Telegraph*, 1 December 1993.

Since this cartoon was published in 1994 there have been two legal landmarks with regard to pregnancy and the interpretation of the Sex Discrimination Act of 1975. At the end of 1995 it was recognized that to dismiss a woman, or to subject her to any detriment because she is pregnant, or in respect of any matter relating to her pregnancy, is unlawful, and she is entitled to compensation, including compensation for injury to feelings, if she is so treated. In the case of *Webb* v. *EMO Cargo (UK) Ltd* (1995), the European Court ruled that to dismiss a woman because she was pregnant was unlawful and offended practice. This ruling has had an impact on cases brought by women who had been dismissed from the armed forces, the Government conceding that they had acted unlawfully. Substantial awards, the largest being half a million pounds, have been made to women pursuing these claims against the Ministry of Defence before an industrial tribunal.

52. Kate Charlesworth, *Fast Forward*, Edinburgh District Council's Women's Employment Education and Training Forum, Autumn 1994.

Kate Charlesworth was commissioned to draw this for the Women's Employment and Technical Forum of Edinburgh District Council quarterly newsletter, illustrating an article titled 'Euro Court Rules in Favour of Women'. She says that this cartoon reflects her belief that 'women will never achieve equality in the workplace as long as men see our gender as a disqualification'. Her lines and shapes and solid inking are as assured as anybody's.

69

Mrs Thatcher used her handbag as a weapon. Harold and his friend are still schoolboys with pens and conkers and sticky buns in their pockets. In the Eighties 'power suits' dealt with the perceived problem of women's office uniform by feminizing men's suits and adding larger and larger shoulder pads.

This cartoon originated as one of five or six Jacky Fleming was asked to draw to accompany a report on women in the publishing industry. She says:

I was given the text to read, then left to devise appropriate images. I don't enjoy working when people prescribe the image and caption they want. That's an illustrator's job, not a cartoonist's . . . This particular drawing was influenced by a Daumier print which has been hanging in my parents' house all my life. It's a beautiful drawing of two lawyers. I find it strange how images stick in your subconscious and resurface in the most unexpected way.

53. Jacky Fleming, in *A Case of Covert Discrimination*, 1995.

3 | Sharing the Caring

It has been a man's world up to now. Men have been out and about, have smoked pipes, cigars and cigarettes, have drunk and gambled and whored and worked and ruled and preached and judged. When women began to question their roles as wives and mothers, men were horrified, and drew them as cantankerous women aspiring to be men, rather than aspiring to men's freedom.

The image of woman in the Protestant and Catholic churches is based on a virgin mother; the charismatic leaders, however, were solitary, celibate men. This model was and is used in worship, song, story, plays and pictures to reinforce women's position in a merely domestic, arid and unfulfilling role as an extra in the wide-screen film that is life.

In the period we are looking at women are caricatured as shrews, absurdly fashionable, downtrodden housewives, aggressive, stupid and pathetic when drawn by men. By the time women get a chance to hold the pen, and hold the page, we are given much more amusing and spunky role models. Women can now be seen as sexy predators, dry wits, realists in the face of male fantasy, and winners in the battle of the sexes that men started in the first place.

And as the century progresses we begin to see caricatures of the bigoted male position, with twerps and colonels and Andy Capp, and that terrible rogues' gallery of boozers, trendy vicars, drippy polytechnic lecturers and Masters of the Double Standard in the great satires of Posy Simmonds.

Feminist cartooning has come of age. It is an irony that I have discovered that many of these female comic stars are sharing the caring at home, which can be anywhere in the country, working with the fax and the phone, and sabotaging the status quo in child-caring and child-sharing while holding kids in one hand and art pens in the other. The technology of the press has helped these independent women, home-workers we can call them, to carry the battle for equality into every paper and magazine and every house in the land. The press is still male-dominated. These women are not given enough space – but they are fierce and funny, and they take the fight to the enemy and challenge clichéd, blinkered thinking by men. Women are for learning and love and life, like men – but they can bear children as well. If men want children, they should look after them.

54. Howard Somerville,
Punch, 25 January 1905.

PRIMUM VIVERE, DEINDE PHILOSOPHARI.

"Is FLORRIE'S ENGAGEMENT REALLY OFF, THEN?"

"OH, YES. JACK WANTED HER TO GIVE UP GAMBLING AND SMOKING, AND GOODNESS KNOWS WHAT ELSE." (*Chorus.*) "HOW ABSURD!!"

The women depicted opposite are 'fast', glamorous, louche 'New Women'. A rough translation of their Latin motto: 'First live, then philosophize.' Women smoking and gambling is a reversal of gender roles, and to most Edwardians such reversals were 'unwomanly', 'unsexing', and threatening. It was assumed that roles would have to reverse in order to accommodate a change in women's position, not that new habits could be added to the repertoire of women's roles. Women smoking was disturbingly erotic, bohemian, not widely seen for another ten years, during the First World War. Florrie eschewing marriage, then considered the only possible career for a woman, in favour of smoking and gambling, would have sent a *frisson* through the Edwardian male society.

Published in 1905, this cartoon was drawn when the suffragettes' militant campaign for the vote was at its earliest stage. It predates the first militant act, at a political meeting at the Free Trade Hall in Manchester, which saw Christabel Pankhurst and Annie Kenney thrown out of the building for interrupting the speakers and asking several times when the Government would give women the vote. They continued their protest outside and were arrested and sent to Strangeways Prison for seven days and three days respectively. The Women's Social and Political Union was almost eighteen months old.

Howard Somerville was a painter, etcher and illustrator. Born in 1873 in Dundee, he abandoned his studies in science and engineering to become an artist. He died in 1940.

The belief that 'a woman's place is in the home' seems to date from the eighteenth century. Some Christians believed that God had divided the world into two spheres: the public and the private. The public world of work and politics was men's sphere, and the private world of hearth and home was women's sphere. This 'domestic ideology' underpinned British society until recent times, and in some quarters still does.

This Catherine Courtauld cartoon was published as a poster and as a postcard. Courtauld was born in 1878 and died in 1972; her brother was Samuel Courtauld, who was the head of the Courtauld textile business. She designed a number of images for the Atelier.

Our understanding of prehistoric women's lives has been recently revised, presenting more varied roles for women such as tool-making, metal-working, pottery and particularly agriculture: one of the foundations of culture and social progress.

55. Catherine Courtauld,
The Suffrage Atelier, 1912.

Her man is three pets and a smoking lamp: he is three kinds of animal and a machine that does not work. She is sublime and he is a mess. Donald McGill (1875–1962) designed this postcard, which was published in the 'Funny Parrot' and 'Matrimonial Comic' series. Sending a card like this was a chance for a woman on holiday to criticize men, or her husband, while writing home.

McGill's work of the Thirties through to the Sixties earned him the title 'King of the Saucy Postcards'. (He was even prosecuted in the Fifties under the 1857 Obscene Publications Act.) McGill studied at Blackheath Art School and then went to work in the drawing office of a firm of naval architects, becoming a cartoonist and postcard designer in 1908. Some of his earliest images were commissioned by the opponents of women's suffrage. In 1941 George Orwell wrote of McGill: 'He is not only the most prolific and by far the best of contemporary postcard artists, but also the most representative, the most perfect in the tradition.' Orwell, who was a great journalist, thought that McGill could not be one artist, but the name for a group of artists in a studio. They both lived in London at the same time: Orwell could have telephoned McGill and asked him.

56. Donald McGill, Inter-Art, 1919.

" Why should I want a husband ? I've got a parrot that swears, a dog that growls, a lamp that smokes—and a cat that stops out all night ! "

75

It is 1929 and divorce is in fashion: women are queueing up to divorce their husbands. Earlier, the Matrimonial Causes Act of 1923 had allowed women to divorce their husbands for adultery, abolishing the double standard in divorce whereby men could divorce their wives for adultery, but women could not divorce their husbands on similar grounds. The Guardianship of Infants Act of 1925 gave mothers rights as guardians of their own children for the first time; until then fathers had been the sole guardians. In England and Wales the number of petitions for divorce went from 2,907 in 1921 to 5,903 in 1937, the year of the new Matrimonial Causes Act, when cruelty and wilful desertion by the husband became grounds for divorce. Between 1926 and 1930, 59 per cent of divorces were instigated by women. To put the changing pattern of divorce in a wider historical context: in 1911, 1 in 500 marriages ended in divorce; in 1937, it was 1 in 60; in 1954, 1 in 15, and if divorce rates remain unchanged at their 1993–4 level, it is estimated that 4 in 10 of current marriages will eventually end in divorce.

The *Evening Standard*'s editorial that day was 'Fair Play for Husbands', and gave details about Mr and Mrs G's marital difficulties. Mr Justice Hill's decision in the Divorce Court has done

something towards clearing the general muddle in which matrimony legally lies in these days of the uneven emancipation of women. Mrs G sued her husband for restitution of conjugal rights because he refused either to take her to live with him abroad, where his prosperous business was, or to come and make a living in England. Mr G's defence was that his wife's extravagance had been such that a condition of his holding his foreign position was that he should not be in the same neighbourhood [as her], and he provided her with an allowance of £2,400 a year. Mr Justice Hill dismissed Mrs G's claim on the ground that any husband, being bound to maintain his wife and children, must be allowed to choose where and how he will earn a living. If the place and the means do not allow his wife to live with him, then his separation from her does not make him guilty of desertion ... But only those of us with a very limited contact with the world will be unable to recall in our own experience cases of wives who by their fantastic conduct of one sort or another have improved or defeated their husbands' professional careers without ever giving their victims legal ground for divorce, or by threats of such conduct have been able to lead them here and there in a kind of highly varnished slavery. The wide publicity of Mr Justice Hill's decision may have been [*sic*] a good educational effect on many such women (who often live in the delightful delusion that they are perfectly good and incalculably precious wives) and put courage into the hearts of victimized men.

Wives cannot have it both ways. They now have the assurance that their husbands are legally responsible for their maintenance and for that of their children. They cannot be compelled to live with their husbands against their wills. That they should also have power to force their husbands now east, now west, according to their whims, would be intolerable injustice to women in general, it must be owned that very few of them do desire any such complete legal enslavement of men.

In Low's cartoon there are no men, only Cupid and the bell-boy, but there are all sorts of women of all ages. They are wives waiting to remove Cupid's arrow; a couple of them have brought fold-up chairs to wait as if for the start of the January Sales.

There is a powerful contrast between the position of married women in 1929 and that of Victorian women, some of whom were sold by their husbands, often with a tether round their neck, at Smithfield Market in London. Before 1857 the only way to get a divorce was by

57. David Low, *Evening Standard*, 16 November 1929.

THE QUEUE ENTERTAINER.

an Act of Parliament, which was an expensive and slow business. The Matrimonial Causes Act (1857) allowed divorce through the law courts. A husband only had to prove his wife's adultery, but a wife could divorce her husband on the grounds of (proven) adultery, incest, bigamy, cruelty or desertion. Divorce was still expensive and by no means universally affordable, and many couples who were unhappy together and unable to afford to divorce often agreed to the illegal, but, in certain parts of the country, quite common, practice of wife-selling.

It is traditional for men to take off their shoes to creep up the stairs after a night in the pub. Here the roles are reversed – it is one o'clock and she is making the old excuse that she has been working late. The year is 1943 and she has clearly been out on the town. He clutches his dressing gown to his throat in the classic 'What time do you call this' pose.

This cartoon is the work of 'Maroc' (Robert S. E. Coram), whose name is also a reversal. Not much is known about him except that he flourished in the Thirties and Forties. He studied at Goldsmith's College in the evenings. *Punch*, the *Evening Standard* and *Men Only* also published his work.

58. 'Maroc' (Robert S. E. Coram), *Sheffield Telegraph*, 23 October 1943.

'I'm sorry, dear, I was working late at the factory.

his cartoon by Reg Smythe features an absent Florrie Capp
who controls the purse strings. The pub and drink are often
a contested area for the Capps. Andy Capp thinks that money
spent on drink and socializing is spent seriously, not frittered away. He
can attack his wife's attitude with words, but she acts by denying him.

59. Reg Smythe, *The Andy Capp Book, Daily Mirror,* 1958.

'Not today, Percy,

Florrie frittered the money away

on food an' rent.'

ndy Capp is solicitous – up to a point. He loves his wife within his belief system. He wears his cap and muffler, she has her apron, her 'pinny'. His cap is his symbol of authority, the 'pinny' is hers. Andy Capp is taken from 'handicap', a horse-racing term: he has a handicap in the rigidity of his unreconstructed male response which he transcends with his unconscious humour. Flo or Florrie, an old-fashioned name made popular by the nineteenth-century nurse Florence Nightingale, was the name of Reg Smythe's mother.

60. Reg Smythe, *The Andy Capp Book*, *Daily Mirror*, 1958.

'*Yer look proper poorly. Florrie, don't yer bother about the washin'-up tonight – do it in the mornin'.*'

Ford car-worker's wife as 'sweater-girl' and dominatrix. It is 1962 and some Ford workers' wives have held a meeting to discuss whether their husbands should go on strike or not. The *Daily Mail*, publisher of this 'Emmwood' cartoon, also asked, 'How much does the contemporary wife dominate the contemporary husband?' and quoted social scientists' recent claims that 'the dominant position of the male shows signs of being challenged. 'Fighting Mad: The Ford Wives' was the headline to an anti-trade union and misogynistic story, describing the efforts of three Ford car-workers' wives who had called a meeting of wives in Dagenham:

The experience of a hundred and fifty wives sitting and arguing politely with just the occasional heated discussion, turned out to be . . . well, what any *man* could have forecast anyway . . . The feudin' and the fightin', the accusations and the demands, the tears and the anger lasted at the meeting about an hour. It continued afterwards. The end came with a remark that a student of women's emancipation might care to analyse: 'Lord, my husband will want his tea.' And they all went home.

61. 'Emmwood' (John Musgrave-Wood), *Daily Mail*, 14 November 1962.

Jackie Kennedy is a model for the woman in this drawing. 'Emmwood' (John Musgrave-Wood) is the cartoonist. Born in 1915, Musgrave-Wood studied at Leeds College of Art and later at Goldsmith's. He drew for *Punch* and the *Sunday Express*, and then the *Evening Standard*. He became the Political Cartoonist at the *Daily Mail* in 1957, retiring in 1975.

WHO REALLY RULES THE ROOST IN YOUR HOUSE?

The sight of Ford wives holding a meeting on whether their husbands should go on strike or not prompts a question: how much does the contemporary wife dominate the contemporary husband?

Social scientists claim that the dominant position of the male shows signs of being challenged. In Britain the male still tends to be in command in the North, while the female is gaining ground in the South.

How is the sex war going in your household? The following questionnaire has been designed according to psychological tests for dominance or submissiveness.

1. If you have a party of 'people in', are the introductions done by
   (a) *your wife?*
   (b) *you?*
   (c) *both of you?*

2. If you have a row
   (a) *do you generally storm out, leaving her?*
   (b) *does she storm out, leaving you?*
   (c) *do you both stay put, battling until the end?*

3. Is (a) *your wife – unlike you – always joining things: associations, societies, CND marches, twist clubs, bingo?*
   Or (b) *are you – unlike her – always joining things: T. A., British Legion, working men's clubs, etc.?*
   Or (c) *are you both 'joiners' or 'non-joiners'?*

4. Is (a) *your wife always saying 'now, look here, let's have this out'?*
   Are (b) *you always saying it?*
   Are (c) *you both always saying it?*

5. Do you feel that
   (a) *your wife is too impetuous?*
   (b) *she always takes too long making up her mind?*
   (c) *she is a model of discretion?*

6. When the housekeeping was considered, did you
   (a) *ask her how much she wanted?*
   (b) *tell her how much she was getting?*
   (c) *decide to have a common account?*

7. If you buy a car, who will have the biggest say in the choice
   (a) *your wife?*
   (b) *you?*
   (c) *the salesman?*

8. When you find yourselves thrown in with a bunch of strangers
   (a) *does your wife do the talking?*
   (b) *do you do the talking?*
   (c) *don't either of you talk to strangers?*

9. Do you notice that people keep coming for help and advice to
   (a) *your wife, but not to you?*
   (b) *you, but not your wife?*
   (c) *neither of you, or both?*

10. Do you feel that
    (a) *your wife is a bit too fond of competing with the neighbours?*
    (b) *you would like your wife to show a little more ambition?*
    (c) *you make a comfortable, easy-going team?*

★

The A's point to a dominant wife, the B's to a dominant husband, the C's to a state of marital equilibrium. Add up your score and draw your own conclusions!

Emmwood.

Role reversal as perceived in 1971. Kenneth Mahood, who was born in Belfast in 1930, has imagined a world where women, typified by Myra Grimshaw, are the bosses and have taken on the roles and selfish and inconsiderate behaviour of men. Mahood's sleek modern line is suggestive of movement and ambition – suited to a businesswoman's life, somewhat.

From 1948 he contributed regularly to *Punch*, becoming Assistant Art Editor in 1960 until 1965. He was Political Cartoonist on *The Times* in the late Sixties and also drew for the *Financial Times* from 1972 to 1982. the *Daily Mail* has published his work since 1982.

62. Kenneth Mahood, *Punch*, 26 May 1971.

osy Simmonds uses her special visual skills to get us to read a text. Her picture is of a bedraggled mother showing the professional mothers in the advertisement, but the writing packs the punch. In a tremendous piece of irony, Simmonds is saying that being a mother is like soldiering – which involves being dirty, a tight routine and discipline; occasionally it has its moments of awful danger; and you always have to be aware of your charges. In fact, being a mother is much more important than being a soldier. It is a job which has always attracted criticism and immense complications, and by referring to a contemporary Army recruiting poster campaign of the Seventies, Simmonds shows up the regard in which advertising men hold soldiers in comparison to the way in which they represent mothers. She says:

I began doing pocket cartoons – simple drawings and short captions. When it came to doing the *Guardian* strip, the space seemed gigantic – needed filling up with words and detail. I have continued words and detail ever since.

63. Seventies Army
recruiting poster.

Is your job getting you anywhere?

Right now we're at work in Canada, Cyprus, Germany and Hong Kong.

Have you been anywhere special lately? Or would you like to write off what you're doing as a bad job and start again?

Well, if we see eye to eye, we can offer you a career. There are over 200 opportunities on offer.

You want to get your HGV? We're looking out for the right sort of men.
You're interested in engineering?
You could have the talent to build our bridges. Perhaps you've got a gift, but don't know it, for the technical side.

We could train you to be a radar operator, a welder, a vehicle mechanic. We'll also ask you to do a four month tour in Northern Ireland. But that still gives us plenty of time to get you to plenty of other places.

And the quicker you get on, the sooner we'll recognise it. We've got lance corporals on £38 a week at 18. Corporals on

£48 a week at 19. Sergeants on £55 a week at the ripe old age of 23. We leave you with this invitation.

If you're honest enough to admit you're stuck in a groove, see how we can get you out of it.

Contract	Starting pay	After six months
3 years	£26.22	£28.95
6 years	£28.32	£31.05
9 years	£31.47	£34.20

The Professionals.

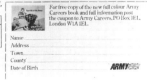

For free copy of the new full colour Army Careers book and full information post the coupon to Army Careers, PO Box 1EL, London W1A 1EL.

Name
Address
Town
County
Date of Birth   ARMY

64. Posy Simmonds,
Guardian, 1977.

Sunday lunch is a British tradition: church first, then roast meat and two vegetables. Men are the architects and women the builders of this ritualized institution. Men's and children's appetites have taken priority in many homes. As long as I can remember, my mother would always say 'Give your Dad the leg [of chicken]', I had the breast and she always had the miserable wings. Women have to use their time preparing the Sunday lunch; men, the 'breadwinners', just sit down to eat it. The caption refers to the phrase 'One man's meat is another man's poison': it is like poison to lose your Sundays in this way. Claude Lévi-Strauss argues that cooking is not biologically necessary but should be seen as a way of adding culture to the food we consume.

Mel Calman (1931–94) was born in London and went to St Martin's School of Art and Goldsmith's College. He cartooned for the *Daily Express* (1957–1963), the *Sunday Telegraph* (1964–65), the *Observer* (1965–66), the *Sunday Times* (1979–84) and *The Times* (1979–94). He also produced cartoons on 'Men and Women' for the Field Newspaper Syndicate in America. He later wrote:

I felt excited and terrified … it felt like being something very close to a professional – and the thought kept me awake at night. I preferred to think of myself as a gifted amateur – a man who had somehow managed to get his work printed, in spite of his failings.

65. Mel Calman, in *The Framing of the Female*, Pat Barr, Kestrel Books, 1978

Germaine Greer, and others, have asked the question 'Why aren't there more women artists?' Many women writers have had to balance their writing with household chores and child-care. Some women do their own work when their children are older. Sylvia Plath killed herself with one of housework's central objects, a gas cooker. This Mel Calman drawing telescopes the frustration of ambition by other people's demands. Domestic chores are not finite: women artists and writers have to snatch time to pursue their own work.

This cartoon is the frontispiece to Pat Barr's *The Framing of the Female* (1978). She contends that:

We have an 'allotted space' in time and space. The space we are allotted is not only physical; it is also psychological, emotional, mental – that which gives an individual room to manoeuvre, to exercise his or her own abilities and inclinations. This is inner space – where others impinge, direct, challenge, in the wider world, in everyday social intercourse, in work, in various forms of community and public life. The spaces we are allotted are framed, with varying degrees of rigidity, by the conventions, prejudices, expectations and laws of the society in which we live.

66. Mel Calman, in
The Framing of the Female,
Pat Barr, Kestrel Books,
1978.

87

He is telling her they have a perfect marriage after she has told him she wants a divorce. You get a glimpse of the inner workings of a marriage here because he says that by asking she is 'whining', which implies repetition. In his vision she is like a child asking again and again. He is ignoring her by reading the newspaper which relates to the big external world. He wears his striped City shirt and his City spectacles. She is marooned in her armchair.

Sally Artz was born in 1935 and studied graphic design at St Martin's School of Art. Her work has been published in *Punch*, *Sunday People*, *TitBits*, the *Daily Mirror*, *Private Eye*, *Bella*, *Reader's Digest* and *Chat*. This piece was done 'on spec'. With Artz the idea always comes first, before the caption:

I then set to work honing these until they are as good as I can get them. Then I do the drawing – quickly! I'd say cartooning is more akin to comedy script-writing than to so-called 'fine art' . . . I am a professional cartoonist. I just try to think up funny ideas. My attitudes don't really come into it.

She thinks that 'most cartoonists don't *change* attitudes – they *reflect* them.' Artz has been influenced by the work of Nicholas Bentley and Chon Day.

'*We have a perfect marriage. Why spoil it by whining for a divorce?*'

67. Sally Artz, *Punch*, 17 January 1979.

One man's idiosyncrasies are another person's nightmares. As we are not told what the grounds for divorce are we can imagine them to be either unspeakable acts or tiny *faux pas*. He has the newspaper that men have, and he is in front of the armchair, a kind of throne. Her posture is eloquently drawn.

Merrily Harpur drew this cartoon 'on spec'. She was born in 1948 and studied English at Trinity College, Dublin. Before joining the *Guardian* in 1978 as a writer and cartoonist, she was a restorer of oil paintings. Michael Heath is her favourite cartoonist. She says that none of her cartoons reflect her attitudes: 'I have not got attitudes – I'm a professional cartoonist.'

68. Merrily Harpur, *Punch*, 17 January 1979.

'What do you mean, grounds for divorce?
Those are my idiosyncrasies!'

When women become housewives and mothers, they are often turning their backs on all kinds of jobs, including – as illustrated here by Merrily Harpur – the job of surgeon. It is difficult to go back to high-powered jobs because the technology and practises move on so quickly. Is this cartoon a fantasy? Women in the professions have, and have always had, help with housework and childcare – whether they have been using labour-saving machines or nannies – and the jingle for a washing-up liquid commercial has hardly been relevant to their lives.

The statistics for women in surgical specialities speak for themselves. In 1993, out of 103 neurosurgery consultants, only one was a woman (1 per cent); in general surgery, out of 1,054 consultants there were only 16 women (1.5 per cent). The highest percentage of women (18 per cent) was found in paediatric surgery where they numbered 9 out of the 50 consultants. Before 1950 only 22 women were Fellows of the Royal College of Surgeons; between 1950 and 1959 the figure was 42; from 1960 to 1969 there were 58; 1970 to 1979 saw the numbers rise to 89; by the end of 1989 there were 157, and in 1990 there were 165.

The Part-Time Consultants' Scheme is an Opportunity 2000 initiative designed to create new part-time posts for doctors who are unable to work full-time. So far 120 part-time consultants are on this scheme, of whom 115 are female (96 per cent). In other words, less than 4 per cent of all female consultants, and less than 1 per cent of all consultants work part-time.

69. Merrily Harpur, *Punch*, 22 October 1980.

'Yes, darling! Mummy has to keep her hands lovely in case she ever wants to go back to brain surgery.'

ike many classical sculptures, the Venus de Milo has lost her arms. Here, transformed into the Venus de Lino, she has stepped off her plinth, and, with her one miraculously regained arm, is cleaning the floor. The roles which women fulfil are diverse and extreme – from goddesses to cleaners.

Paula Youens drew this cartoon for a solo exhibition. 'Venus de Lino' was one of a series of cartoons on housework and women's work. Youens feels that 'cartoons are very accessible, easily absorbed and powerful images which can make people think, and that's the first step towards changing opinions and ideas'. Claire Brétecher and Christine Roche are two cartoonists who have influenced her. 'Venus de Lino' reflects her attitudes to 'housework, childcare and cleaning, which are still thought of as women's work. It's been a long, hard battle.'

70. (Below) The first-century BC statue called the Venus de Milo was once part of a group of figures which included Cupid, towards whom the Venus stretched her arms.

71. (Below right) Paula Youens, in *Lone Thoughts From A Broad*, The Women's Press, 1981.

The washing machine has qualities that are probably lacking in this housewife's male partner. Like a lot of women working in the home, the woman portrayed in this Viv Quillin cartoon suffers from loneliness and frustration, which drives her to talk to herself, and, alarmingly, fall in love with a machine. In many households 'white goods' – dishwashers, refrigerators and washing machines – are seen as being in the female domain, whereas black and chrome items such as televisions, video-recorders and compact-disc players are seen as the male preserve.

72. Viv Quillin, in *Women's Work*, Hamish Hamilton, 1984.

Her head is lower than a doormat. She hides like an ostrich is said to do. This is a conflation of the 'Welcome' mat and the 'Home Sweet Home' embroidered samplers of Victorian and Edwardian times. All the objects are signs: the pram; the cooker, the iron, the baby's bottle, the broom and the dustpan. There is a hidden man sitting in an armchair reading the newspaper, as usual.

Christine Roche says this drawing is about

women who stick their heads in the sand and conform . . . I don't think that cartooning changes anything, but it will reinforce an existing or emerging point of view. I came to cartooning out of necessity (earning a living) and politics (the left and feminism). I remember loving Fougasse when I was very young.

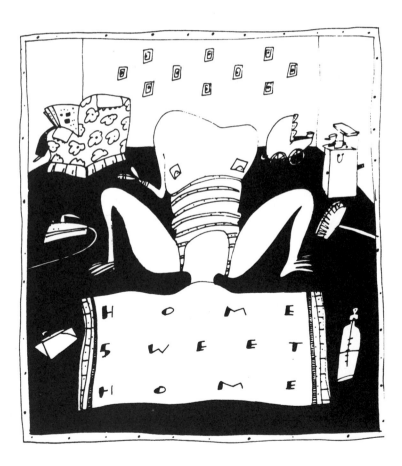

73. Christine Roche, in *"I'm not a feminist but ..."*, Virago Press, 1985.

93

It is their baby but only one person needs to get up. Which one? A lot of evidence suggests that mothers get up in the night because 'fathers have to get up for work in the morning'. There is a long history of childcare being avoided, or often extremely unequally shared, or put into the hands of underpaid and undervalued childminders and nannies.

Caroline Firenza (her '*nom de* felt tip') was born in 1950 in Kent. She trained as a graphic designer and started to draw, cartoon and illustrate as a 'more effective and cheaper alternative to photographs'. She lives and works in Sheffield and drew this for a work colleague whose wife had just had a baby. She believes that cartooning can lead to change:

The facility to isolate and concentrate on something can help change the way we look at and understand things ... I have children – [this cartoon is] just a glimpse of real life – but more real than normal baby cards ... I do a lot of work as an illustrator and tend to concentrate more on visual humour than adding captions ... As I get older, I see more of the world and still spend most of my energy debunking male (most usually) pomposity and assumed positions.

Firenza's favourite cartoonists include: Hector Breeze, Claire Brétecher, 'ffolkes', Giles, Merrily Harpur, Michael Heath, Posy Simmonds and Bill Tidy.

74. Caroline Firenza, Graphics Equalizer, 1986.

94

The Victorian game of Happy Families is played roughly like this: three or more players ask each other if cards showing particular family members (there are nine families of four) are 'at home' (in an opponent's hand); if the answer is yes, the player who asks may take that card into his or her hand. The Baker's family shown overleaf is a typical Happy Family. Posy Simmonds's own version of these apparently unchanging nuclear families in an unchanging world of butchers and bakers and candlestick-makers is used both visually and verbally to remark 'how different life is' from the card game – and from Mrs Thatcher's dream of a bourgeois Britain, based on Victorian values. Around the time this cartoon was published Mrs Thatcher famously said that there was no such thing as society: presumably there were only individuals and families with no social ties or social responsibilities, as is subtly hinted at in the cartoon. In April 1993 the Child Support

75. Posy Simmonds, *Guardian*, 1987.

95

Agency was set up to make separated or divorced fathers pay something towards the upkeep of their children. In 1994–5 there were in Britain 1.5 million lone parents bringing up 2.3 million children. In total 23 per cent of all families with dependent children were headed by a lone parent. Simmonds's combination of good humour, strong satire and brilliant story-telling about what is happening off-camera, in the real world, makes her arguably the greatest contemporary strip cartoonist.

76. 'Happy Families' card game of the 1890s.

t is after a dinner party, in a house without a dishwasher. The woman demonstrates that the dirty plates do not own her, she owns
them. Her extravagance is a protest against the need to wash up after
cooking and serving a meal for a large number of people. The visitors
have gone out into the night and she is chucking their rubbish after
them. This Jacky Fleming cartoon reminds us of the feelings one has
after such an occasion. The party is an experience, not a thing, but one
is left with mere things – dirty dishes. It is said that the surrealist artist
René Magritte would often, out of sheer naughtiness, drop plates on
to the floor – where they broke – when he was washing up.

Fleming comments:

I think that anything which touches people's hearts can bring about change.
You can shift someone's perceptions and understanding, and you can puncture
long-held beliefs; you can break taboos; you can provoke a change of heart;
you can provide hope or solidarity; you can focus on an issue; you can create
doubt where there was only certainty; you can make folly or injustice visible;
you can provoke laughter.

77. Jacky Fleming, in *Be a
Bloody Train Driver*, Penguin
Books, 1991.

97

The job is being a mother and coping with the ingratitude of children. One can end up concentrating on the bathwater rather than the baby. With modern appliances, is the job easier, or does it simply extend in different ways? Cleanliness is not next to happiness: there are dirty, untidy and even ill-fed families who are happy and fulfilled.

Rona Chadwick believes that feminist cartooning 'changes things':

Firstly, it articulates feminist women's culture in a way that promotes sisterhood, raises our spirit as activists and challenges the 'malestream'. It worries the boys – makes them realize what it's like to be the butt of humour – they don't like it. I always say to them, 'What's wrong with you – haven't you got a sense of humour?' . . . It is only one factor in a complex and dynamic mix of competing tensions. In concert with a range of other feminist change mechanisms, such as stand-up comedy and theory, it is a powerful tool for change. For those people who have already converted, it merely reinforces existing attitudes, hopefully in a way that promotes action and sisterhood.

She has been influenced by Cath Jackson and Angela Martin.

78. Rona Chadwick, in *Hysterical Women: A Collection of 100 Australian Feminist Cartoons*, Women's Electoral Lobby, 1993.

Many familial relationships are circular: the abused abuse others; the battered batter others; the neglected neglect others; and so on. Workshops and family psychotherapy, imported from the United States, have grown significantly in the United Kingdom in the last decade. Jacky Fleming's cartoon brings to mind the first verse of Philip Larkin's poem 'This Be The Verse' (1974):

> They fuck you up, your mum and dad.
> They may not mean to, but they do.
> They fill you with the faults they had
> And add some extra, just for you.

79. Jacky Fleming, in *Never Give Up*, Penguin Books, 1992.

She calls him 'dear' because he is pontificating, the way men do, about where women have gone wrong. She prefers to lose the institution of marriage. This century, the number of couples cohabiting, rather than marrying, has increased hugely. Since the invention of the contraceptive pill, women have been able to control their own fertility and pursue careers in a way unimaginable before the Second World War. The 'marriage bar' prevented many women from working once they got married, although some did marry in secret, only leaving when they became pregnant. However, women's war work was so vital that the belief that a woman's place was in the home was put to one side, as were male sensitivities to comments and accusations that women went out to work because their men could not suppport them, and the 'marriage bar' was dropped during the wars and not reimposed on all professional women after 1945. In the Twenties and Thirties there had been an exception to the bar in the case of women teachers and civil servants, who were allowed to work – but only if their husbands were too ill or disabled to be the traditional breadwinners.

Jacky Fleming says that she finds men in suits 'slightly ridiculous. If people are going to wear the trappings of power, it would help if they were fit to use it. Otherwise they look even more foolish.'

80. Jacky Fleming, in *Never Give Up*, Penguin Books, 1992.

Endpiece

Ludwig Wittgenstein said, 'A serious work in philosophy could be written that consisted entirely of jokes,' but I do not think that a serious work of history could consist entirely of cartoons. *Funny Girls* is a partial history of 130 years of women's hopes and fears. A sea of ink has flowed, and forests have been felled, to produce millions of sketchy stereotypes – *Funny Girls* is only a tiny fraction – which stand for so many different attitudes. I imagine thousands of nibs jabbing at paper like so many fingers stabbing the air to argue the toss.

'Funny' men are the problem that *Funny Girls* is about. We all know that women can do everything that men can do. But we still find that women are discriminated against at work and in the political process. Wise women and men will go on making jokes about the narrow-mindedness and foolishness of the status quo, which restricts so many women's lives. And pens are still poised, cartoons still drawn to illustrate women's struggle for equality and fulfilment.

As the collector and curator of this cabinet of curiosities, I hope that this book will, subtly or hugely, change your outlook on women's lives, and, in some way, change you.

Bibliography

Adams, Carol, *Ordinary Lives a Hundred Years Ago*, Virago Press, 1982

Atkinson, Diane, *Votes for Women*, Cambridge University Press, 1988
  The Suffragettes in Pictures, Sutton Publishing and Museum of London, 1996

Baker, Kenneth, *The Prime Ministers: An Irreverent Political History in Cartoons*, Thames and Hudson, 1995

Banks, Olive, *The Biographical Dictionary of British Feminists, Volume 1: 1800–1930*, Wheatsheaf Books, 1983

Barr, Pat, *The Framing of the Female*, cartoons by Mel Calman, Kestrel Books, 1978

Bolt, Christine, *The Women's Movements in the United States and Britain from the 1790s to the 1920s*, Harvester Wheatsheaf, 1993

Bozdan, Pamela, Factsheet no. 5: *Women in the House of Commons*, 1988, revised by John Prince, House of Commons, 1995

Braybon, Gail, *Women Workers in the First World War*, Croom Helm, 1981

Braybon, Gail and Summerfield, Penny, *Out of the Cage: Women's Experiences in Two World Wars*, Pandora Press, 1987

Bryant, Mark and Heneage, Simon (compilers), *Dictionary of British Cartoonists and Caricaturists, 1730–1980*, Scolar Press, 1994

Calder-Marshall, Arthur, *Wish You Were Here: The Art of Donald McGill*, Hutchinson and Co., 1966

Calman, Mel, *But it's my turn to leave you ...*, Methuen, 1980
  Calman Revisited, Methuen, 1983
  A Little Light Worrying: The Best of Mel Calman, Methuen, 1996

Condell, Diana and Liddiard, Jean, *Working for Victory: Images of Women in the First World War, 1914–1918*, Routledge & Kegan Paul, 1987

Cook, Chris and Stevenson, John, *The Longman Handbook of Modern British History, 1714–1980*, Longman, 1983

Crawford, Anne, Hayter, Tony, Hughes, Ann, Prochaska, Frank, Stafford, Pauline, Vallance, Elizabeth (editors), *The Europa Biographical Dictionary of British Women: Over 1,000 Notable Women from Britain's Past*, Europa Publications, 1983

Davidson, C., *A Woman's Work is Never Done: The History of Housework in the British Isles, 1650–1950*, Chatto & Windus, 1986

Duff, Peggy, *Left, Left Left: A Personal Account of Six Protest Campaigns, 1945–1965*, Allison & Busby, 1971

Forster, Margaret, *Significant Sisters: Grassroots of Active Feminism, 1839–1939*, Secker and Warburg, 1984

Garrett Fawcett, Millicent, *The Women's Victory and Afterwards: Personal Reminiscences, 1911–1918*, Sidgwick & Jackson, 1920

What I Remember, T. Fisher Unwin, 1924

Hammerton, A. James, *Cruelty and Companionship: Conflict in Nineteenth-Century Married Life*, Routledge, 1992

Holdsworth, Angela, *Out of the Doll's House: The Story of Women in the Twentieth Century*, BBC Books, 1988

Horn, Pamela, *Women in the 1920s*, Alan Sutton Publishing, 1995

International Who's Who of Women, Europa Publications, 1992

Lewis, Jane, *Women in England, 1870–1950: Sexual Divisions and Social Change*, Wheatsheaf Books, 1984

Liddington, Jill, *The Long Road to Greenham: Feminism and Anti-militarism in Britain Since 1820*, Virago Press, 1989

McDonald, Ian, *Vindication!: A Postcard History of the Women's Movement*, Bellew Publishing Co., 1989

Menefee, Samuel Pyeatt, *An Ethnographic Study of British Popular Divorce*, Basil Blackwell, 1981

Nicholson, Mavis, *What Did You Do in the War, Mummy?: Women in World War II*, Pimlico, 1995

Pankhurst, Christabel, *Unshackled: The Story of How We Won the Vote*, Hutchinson, 1959

Pankhurst, Emmeline, *My Own Story: The Autobiography of Emmeline Pankhurst, 1914*, reprinted Virago Press, 1977

Pankhurst, Sylvia, *The Suffragette Movement, 1931*, reprinted Virago Press, 1977

Pugh, Martin, *Women and the Women's Movement in Britain, 1914–1959*, Macmillan, 1992

Routledge, Paul, *Madam Speaker: The Life of Betty Boothroyd*, Harper-Collins, 1996

Rover, Constance, *The Punch Book of Women's Rights*, Hutchinson and Co., 1967

Sharpe, Sue, *Just Like a Girl: How Girls Learn to be Women*, Penguin Books, 1981

Sheridan, Dorothy, *War Factory: Mass Observation* (Introduction), The Cressett Library, 1987

Sheridan, Dorothy (editor), *Wartime Women: An Anthology of Women's Wartime Writing for Mass Observation, 1937–1945*, Mandarin Paperbacks, 1990

Shils, Edward and Blacker, Carmen (editors), *Cambridge Women: Twelve Portraits*, Cambridge University Press, 1996

Spender, Dale, *There's Always been a Women's Movement in the Twentieth Century*, Pandora Press, 1983

Stanley, Autumn, *Mothers and Daughters of Invention: Notes for a Revised History of Technology*, The Scarecrow Press, 1993

Summerfield, Penny, *Women Workers in the Second World War*, Croom Helm, 1986

Tickner, Lisa, *The Spectacle of Women: Imagery of the Suffrage Campaign, 1907–1914*, Chatto & Windus, 1987

Twinch, Carol, *Women on the Land*, The Lutterworth Press, 1990

Vallance, Elizabeth, *Women in the House: A Study of Women Members of Parliament*, Athlone Press, 1979

White, C., *Women's Magazines, 1693–1968*, Michael Joseph, 1970

Women have come a long way since 1866

never give up

With kind permission of Jacky Fleming

There is still *so much more to do*

- *Equal Pay*
- *Part-time Workers' Rights*
- *Fair Pensions*
- *Child Benefit*
- *Family Friendly Employment*
- *Women in Decisionmaking*

---You can make a difference!---

Count me in to Fawcett

Name

Address

Postcode

Please send me details about

☐ How to join Fawcett ☐ Campaigning for women

I'd like to make a donation:

☐ £15 ☐ £20 ☐ £25 ☐ £50 ☐ Other

Write to Fawcett, Freepost SE 6903, London EC2 2JD

f fawcett

We've been counted in... Victoria Wood, Jane Lapotaire, Helena Kennedy, Jo Brand, Germaine Greer, Suzanne Moore, Valerie Amos...